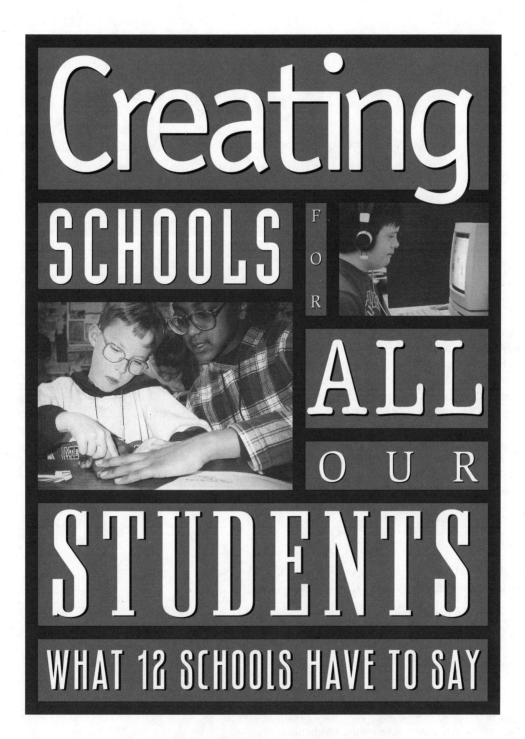

Creating SCHOOLS for ALL OUR STUDENTS

WHAT 12 SCHOOLS HAVE TO SAY

A Product of the Working Forum on Inclusive Schools
Published by The Council for Exceptional Children

An NEA Professional Library Publication
National Education Association
Washington, D.C.

Library of Congress Cataloging-in-Publication Data

Creating schools for all our students: what 12 schools
    have to say : a product of the Working Forum on In-
    clusive Schools.
        p.   cm.
    ISBN 0-86586-255-9
    1. Mainstreaming in education—United States—Case
studies. 2. Handicapped children—Education—United
States—Case Studies. 3. Student assistance programs—
United States—Case studies. 4. Mainstreaming in education—Canada—Case Studies. 5. Handicapped
children—Education—Canada—Case Studies. 6. Student
assistance programs—Canada—Case studies. I. Working
Forum on Inclusive Schools (1994 : Washington, D.C.)
II. Council for Exceptional Children.
LC4019. C65   1995
371.9' 046—dc20   94-34954
                                                    CIP

Copyright 1994 by The Council for Exceptional Children,
1920 Association Drive, Reston, Virginia 22091-1589

Permission is granted to sponsoring associations to
reproduce and adapt any portion of this publication.

Stock No. P5064

Printed in the United States of America

10 9 8 7 6 5 4 3 2 1   OCLC# 31077602

Contents

Acknowledgments

We want to express appreciation to Computer Curriculum Corporation, a Simon and Schuster company, whose financial and professional support made this Working Forum possible. Thanks also to the participating associations for their time and effort in planning and executing the project. Special appreciation is extended to the National Education Association for making their facilities available and providing technical and professional support for the event.

Others whose assistance made the Working Forum a success were the facilitators: Marilyn Crocker, Joe Ballard, Marian Ceasor, John DeWitt, Dana Harader, Lynn Malarz, Margaret McLaughlin, Shelia Mingo, and Judy Schrag.

Finally we wish to thank the writer, Karin Chenoweth, for her valuable assistance in synthesizing the discussions and preparing this practical and friendly publication.

Preface

School systems across the country are continuing to restructure their educational programs to achieve better results for increasingly diverse students with complex learning needs, including those with disabilities. Many of these education reform efforts involve school-based strategies to unite special education, other support programs, and general education, and to better serve students and families.

The first step in transforming schools is to focus on a clear purpose—as defined by the community and the state. If the focus is on a single clear purpose—cognitive, affective, and social development—then the schools can be transformed by teachers and principals who know, among other things, how to include students with disabilities into the everyday fabric of the general classroom and general student activities.

Schools will be judged by performance assessment results. Any suggestions for improvement that aren't structured to improve student achievement are a distraction from the larger mission of transforming public education to succeed with every child at a much higher level.

The term *inclusive schools* has come to be used to describe the changes that are occurring within schools and school districts to better coordinate and unify educational programs and services, as well as to transform schools into places where all children, including those with disabilities, belong and can learn at higher levels. An effective inclusive school has been defined as

A diverse problem-solving organization with a common mission that emphasizes learning for all students. It employs and supports teachers and other staff who are committed to working together to create and maintain a climate conducive to learning. The responsibility for all students is shared.

An effective, inclusive school acknowledges that such a commitment requires administrative leadership, ongoing technical assistance, and long-term professional development. Within inclusive schools, there is a shared responsibility for any problem or any success that we have for students in our schools. (Florian, 1993)

In short, an inclusive school has a shared value that promotes a single, coordinated system of education dedicated to ensuring that all students are empowered to become caring, competent, and contributing citizens in an integrated, changing, and diverse society.

What does all this mean for educators and administrators working at the school level who are interested in implementing inclusive school practices? How is a child's experience, both educationally and socially, within an inclusive school different from a traditional school? How can the school principal, classroom teachers, and other staff go about planning and implementing inclusive school strategies? What role do parents have in inclusive schools that is different from that in more traditional schools? What are inclusive schools like? What kinds of inclusive school strategies have been found to be effective?

In response to these and many other questions from schools across the United States and Canada, 10 national associations have committed themselves to providing information about the range of inclusive school issues, problems, and solutions. These national associations, representing the school community, include:

American Association of School Administrators (AASA)

American Federation of Teachers (AFT)

The Council for Exceptional Children (CEC)

The Council of Great City Schools

National Association of Elementary School
Principals (NAESP)

National Association of Secondary School
Principals (NASSP)

National Association of State Directors of
Special Education (NASDSE)

National Association of State Boards of
Education (NASBE)

National Education Association (NEA)

National School Boards Association (NSBA)

The above national associations identified many schools across the country that have struggled with and solved various complex issues related to inclusive schools. Twelve schools were selected to participate in a national Inclusive Schools Working Forum in March 1994 to relate their planning and implementation stories. While the schools selected have many differences they are not a representative sample of the schools and communities of North America. The information generated at this working forum is the focus of this book. Descriptions of the experiences of these 12 schools and school districts across the United States and Canada are included.

The achievements of these 12 schools in integrating students with disabilities into general education classrooms were not realized easily. They invested a great deal of shared hard work and commitments. Nevertheless the road for these schools was not filled in all cases with the obstacles created by the realities of many schools—insufficient resources, large numbers of at risk and troubled children, over crowded classrooms, highly stressed classroom staff, and an inadequate resource delivery system.

It should be noted that the information presented in this book emerged from the interactions of the forum participants and does not necessarily reflect official policies or views of the participating national associations. Since the participating organizations approach the issues from differing perspectives, the reader is encouraged to examine the organization policies and positions provided in the Appendix. Individual associations should be contacted to obtain additional information regarding inclusive schools.

The challenge of improving every school is in the connections between schools and educators. Children and teachers move every year. Considering mobility, plus family changes caused by marriage and divorce, every classroom in every school must be part of a larger transformation—and the unit of transformation is the local school district. Reform, to be real for every single child, must happen to all school systems, not some schools or classrooms on a hit-or-miss basis.

Although each inclusive school will look different, based on the needs of the students enrolled, a number of overriding features characterize inclusive schools:

1. A Sense of Community

An inclusive school has a philosophy and a vision that all children belong and can learn in the mainstream of school and community life. Diversity is valued and celebrated for bringing strength and opportunities for learning. Within an inclusive school everyone belongs, is accepted, and is supported by peers and the adults in the school. This sense of community helps each child develop a sense of self-worth, pride in his or her accomplishments, and mutual respect.

2. Leadership

The principal plays a crucial role in an inclusive school by actively involving and sharing responsibility with the entire school staff in planning and carrying out the strategies that make the school successful.

3. High Standards

Within inclusive schools, all children meet high levels of educational outcomes and high standards of performance that are appropriate to their needs. Levels of achievement, instructional content, and the manner in which instruction is delivered reflect each student's individual needs.

4. Collaboration and Cooperation

An inclusive school encourages students and staff to support one another with such strategies as peer tutoring, buddy systems, cooperative learning, team teaching, co-teaching, teacher-student assistance teams, and other collaborative arrangements.

5. CHANGING ROLES AND RESPONSIBILITIES

An inclusive school changes the old roles of teachers and school staff. Teachers lecture less and assist more, school psychologists work more closely with teachers in classrooms, and every person in the building is an active participant in the learning process.

6. ARRAY OF SERVICES

An inclusive school offers an array of services—health, mental health, and social services—all coordinated with the educational staff.

7. PARTNERSHIP WITH PARENTS

Parents are embraced as equal and essential partners in the education of their children.

8. FLEXIBLE LEARNING ENVIRONMENTS

Children in an inclusive school are not expected to move in lock steps, but rather follow their individual paths to learning. Groupings are flexible, and material is presented in concrete, meaningful ways that emphasize participation. Although there is less reliance on programs that pull children out of classrooms, there are still opportunities for children to receive separate instruction if needed.

9. STRATEGIES BASED ON RESEARCH

Research into how people learn is providing new ideas and strategies for teachers, and an inclusive school incorporates those ideas. Cooperative learning, curriculum adaptation, peer tutoring, direct instruction, reciprocal teaching, social skills training, computer-assisted instruction, study skill training, and mastery learning are some of the practices that have emerged from the latest research and are applied in inclusive schools.

10. NEW FORMS OF ACCOUNTABILITY

An inclusive school relies less on standardized tests, using new forms of accountability and assessment to make sure that each student is progressing towards his or her goal.

11. ACCESS

An inclusive school ensures that students are able to participate in school life by making necessary modifications to the building and by making available appropriate technology that makes participation possible.

12. CONTINUING PROFESSIONAL DEVELOPMENT

An inclusive school enables staff to design and obtain professional development on an ongoing basis so that there is continuous improvement in the knowledge and skills that they can employ to educate students.

Inclusive Schools and How They Begin

CHAPTER 1

Inclusive Schools and How They Begin

An inclusive school is a school where every child is respected as part of the school community, and where each child is encouraged to learn and achieve as much as possible.

To implement inclusive schools requires new thinking about how children learn, how teachers teach, and how schools are organized and administered.

The 12 schools that participated in the March 1994 Working Forum on Inclusive Schools in Washington, D.C., have all begun the process of change toward becoming inclusive schools. None started at the same point and none proceeded in exactly the same way; however, they are all moving in the same direction. Educators from these schools brought their knowledge and experience to the working forum.

Each of the schools that participated in the working forum began the process of becoming an inclusive school for different reasons. For some, it was due to the advocacy of a parent of a child with disabilities. For others, the impetus came from the general or special education staff. For still others, inclusive school strategies were initiated in response to school district or state initiatives.

But no matter what the origin, the result was that people in each school community eventually embraced the view that they needed to create a place where all children could learn and where differences are cherished for the richness that they bring.

> Ready...fire...aim. Get started with what you have and "grow it" from there.
>
> **Brad Clement. Marshalltown. IA**

HOW TWO SCHOOLS BEGAN TO USE AN INCLUSIVE APPROACH

California

A 1st-grade teacher in California was told 4 days before school began that she would have a special child in her classroom. The child's mother wanted him in the neighborhood school, and the school wanted to comply with her wishes.

The teacher's class size was lowered to 32 to accommodate the child, and the teacher was notified that she would have a full-time paraprofessional who would primarily dedicate herself to the special child.

When she called the child's former kindergarten teacher, she was told that the child was "nonverbal and noncompliant."

The teacher realized that she had a challenge ahead. Not only could the child not speak because of a physical disability, but he often deliberately did the opposite of what the teacher told him to do.

The teacher, in her second year of teaching, was idealistic and hopeful. She had gone into teaching after her own children were in high school with the idea that she would provide a warm, nurturing, caring place for children to happily learn—a very different place from the schools she had attended.

But she was not prepared for this. The moment the boy walked into the classroom, he would begin to keen a high-pitched, annoying sound. The other children would hold their ears and rock back and forth to block the sound. The teacher sent the child out of the classroom more often than he was in. She and the paraprofessional had not worked out ahead of time what to do with the student during breaks and lunches, and so they simply took turns supervising him. One day, when the teacher was watching him during a break, she turned away for just a moment. He disappeared and was found 25 minutes later hiding on the stage. For some months, he was suspended.

At the mother's insistence, the first paraprofessional was fired, then the second, and the third. The mother was now bitterly criticizing the teacher. The teacher's dream of providing a welcoming environment for children had been shattered, and her husband urged her to quit her job before her grief destroyed their family.

When the teacher discussed resigning her position with her principal, steps were finally taken to appropriately address the problem. Using federal and state special education funds, the school hired a specialist in inclusive practices, a highly trained special education teacher. She in turn hired and trained a new paraprofessional. The specialist spent a great deal of time with the child. When he began keening, she would take him out of the classroom and tell him that his behavior was unacceptable and that he needed to behave properly before returning to the classroom. She acquired a computer for him, finally providing a means for him to communicate.

Today, this student is in the 5th grade and communicating through his computer, learning and behaving, and a full member of his class. His 1st-grade teacher, who did not quit, follows his progress closely and says that he writes at a "higher level" than her son who is a college student. One of the subjects the elementary student has written about is how important inclusive practices have been for him.

> In order to do inclusion right, it must be done slowly, with a great deal of planning. This planning must include the people that will have daily contact with students with disabilities. Also, it should begin slowly—don't expect everything to happen at once.
>
> **Participant in the working forum**

And so what began as an example of a sure disaster—an unprepared teacher besieged by a child with enormous needs—ends as a story of triumph. However, the first part of the story could have been prevented if effective planning had taken place from the beginning.

The teacher involved should have received information about the nature of the child's disabilities and the behaviors he exhibited, what was possible for him to achieve, and what instructional strategies were needed. From the first day, the teacher should have had a well-trained classroom assistant and the child a computer. Had all of these things been provided, the child, the child's family, classmates, teacher, and paraprofessionals would have undoubtedly had a less stressful year; and they would have finally achieved success much sooner.

Since then, the school district has adopted a 5-year plan, involving the inclusion specialist, staff members, and the teachers' union representatives. The school district refers to the year the nonverbal, noncompliant child was brought into the classroom as "negative year 1 of the 5-year plan."

New Jersey

An elementary school from New Jersey had a long-standing policy of placing its children with severe disabilities in private schools or self-contained special education rooms.

But one day, Kenny's mom requested that Kenny be allowed to attend the regular classroom. Kenny was 7 years old and classified as having multiple disabilities that needed a special setting. He had been in a private school for 2 years. Although his parents had initially welcomed that placement by the school district, they increasingly became concerned that he was isolated from other children in the community; his academic progress was so slow that it seemed impossible that he would ever be "mainstreamed" with nondisabled students. Moreover, he was not learning how to act outside of the special setting.

When Kenny's parents requested that he attend his neighborhood school, the staff's initial reaction was one of surprise and apprehension. His previous school reported that Kenny had no friends, he had difficulty playing with other children, and he tended to wander off if left unattended. In addition, his disorder made him very sensitive to noise and other stimuli.

However, the staff responded to the challenge with interest and enthusiasm and began planning for Kenny's inclusion. An "inclusion team" was formed, consisting of a speech-language specialist, a school psychologist, a learning consultant, a social worker, Kenny's parents, a special education teacher, a grade-level teacher, and a paraprofessional. This team worked out what would be needed for Kenny, including a full-time paraprofessional, staff-wide training, and a carefully modified curriculum. Although it took time, Kenny became part of his class much more quickly than anyone had expected. Furthermore, staff confidently accepted the challenge of working with students with serious disabilities.

Today, 3 years later, Kenny's mother says that "inclusive education has totally changed my son's life." He is accepted and liked by his classmates and now behaves in more appropriate ways, making family life much better. Moreover, he has far exceeded academic expectations and is now learning in several areas at a rate comparable to his peers.

Kenny's success was so great that the school began to include other students who had been in special settings, including a student with cerebral palsy who required a wheelchair, a computer, and a full-time paraprofessional, and a student with serious emotional problems.

The child with serious emotional disabilities came to the school mid-year before his school records were transferred. He had attended the school a year earlier before moving to Florida, and the staff remembered him as an engaging, bright child. However, he returned to them with some serious problems. Although the staff was aware of the problems, the student was placed in a regular 1st-grade classroom. It soon became apparent that the student's behavior was more disruptive and abusive than any the staff had ever experienced. When his records arrived, they indicated that the student had been in a special education program and had "homicidal tendencies" and "suicide ideation."

Rather than demand that the student be removed from the school, the teacher and principal asked for assistance and more support. The principal often ate lunch with the child, and the school psychologist, the special education teacher, and the paraprofessionals spent more time with the boy. With such intensive staff involvement, the child had no opportunity to harm his classmates or interrupt their education, so he was never permanently excluded from the school or classroom.

During the year the child's behavior moderated, and the staff felt that they were achieving real success. When his family moved out of the district, staff members were not relieved and happy, but disappointed.

A Sense of Community

CHAPTER 2

A Sense of Community

If the central principle of inclusive schools is that all children belong as part of the school community, many of the schools found that fostering a sense of community was of utmost importance. Inclusive schools have a sense of interconnectedness among all staff and all children.

Most of the schools participating in the working forum did not have "building a school community" as a goal when they began their inclusive schools venture. But as these school teams concentrated on including children with disabilities in their schools, they found that their schools became more cohesive and collegial. Teachers learned from each other, children saw adults learning from each other, and children began learning more from the teachers and each other. As staff began to understand the power of their school community, they began to more consciously address ways to foster and maintain that sense of community.

The definition of community involves "sharing, participation, and fellowship," something that does not always exist in many schools. Too often, schools are places where professionals do their work alone and in isolation from other professionals. They have little opportunity to engage in professional conversations or "shop talk" that in other professions is a vital way to keep up with the latest developments and thinking. In addition, they do not have the benefit of regular, ongoing

There is an alternative education class in a room on our campus. It houses 25 kids, kindergarten to 6th grade, and has a very unstructured, "family" approach to education. They share our recess and lunch times, assemblies, and events, but—as I've found out—don't feel a real part of our community.

There is also a general education class that has 5 students with disabilities who are fully integrated. They share all recesses, lunch times, assemblies, and events within the school.

At recess yard duty I noticed the fact that the alternative education kids played alone or fought with other classrooms' children. I also noticed that our fully-included students were indistinguishable from the other children—running, eating snacks, and playing with all the other students.

I tried to talk to the alternative education kids one day about their continual fights at recess. "Why don't you play with the kids in my class, or Mrs. _____ and Miss _____ classes? "They call us *retards*" was their reply.

That's when it hit me between the eyes ... whenever we segregate we risk creating a label ... we risk the hurt and separation ... the low-esteem and awful feelings ... and no matter *who* it involves it should never happen.

Michele Brynjulson, Golden View Elementary, San Ramon, CA

consultation with other members of the staff. Often, only the principal has any say about how the school is organized and administered.

The inclusive schools that participated in the working forum have developed a number of different strategies to nurture a feeling of community, beginning with the development of a common vision.

A Common Vision

If the school as a whole shares the vision that all children need to be a respected part of the school community, that vision alone brings its own sense of community. All students are greeted and chatted with, all professionals feel part of the same staff, and all parents feel welcomed and are encouraged to participate.

Arising from such a vision will be numerous specific, practical ways to make sure each student, staff member, and parent feels a part of the community. Some of those ways are described next. Others will emerge in unexpected ways.

Problem-Solving Teams

Almost all the schools participating in the working forum have set up some kind of a building-based team that makes decisions about how students' individual needs will be met. Each school has its own organization and its own name. For example, one school participating in the working forum has a "management" team with teachers and paraprofessionals, the school counselor, a parent, and the principal. Other schools' problem-solving teams might include a communication-disorder specialist, a learning consultant, or a school psychologist. Other names for problem-solving teams include "teacher assistance team" and "learning support team."

No matter how it is organized or what it is called, the problem-solving team meets regularly to plan what is needed for each child with disabilities. Team members work out such issues as whether the child should be in a general classroom for the whole day or part of the day, whether speech therapy should be provided in the student's classroom or whether the student should go to the therapist's office, and so on. More importantly, problem-solving teams determine the type of special instruction and the extent to which it is needed for individual children. When appropriate, other staff members, such as the nurse, communication disorders specialist, and/or other specialists attend meetings to discuss these issues.

In this way, each child with disabilities benefits from the expertise of many members of the school community, each of whom knows something about the child. Team members all develop broader pictures of what each child is capable of

Management Teams

Most schools developing inclusive policies have some sort of management team to make educational decisions about students with disabilities. Each team is made up differently, but some of the people on such teams include:

principal
special education teacher
general education teacher
counselor or school psychologist
parent
paraprofessional
learning consultant

Additional people who might be brought in for specific discussions could be:

school nurse
communication disorder specialist
reading specialist
art teacher
music teacher
physical education teacher

and what each child needs. Students who are not classified as having a disability also benefit; for if they have difficulties, the team is on hand to share information and plan solutions.

Participants in the working forum reported that teams were initially formed as problem-solving mechanisms to address educational issues. But they soon discovered an unexpected side benefit— the teams helped build school-wide consensus on a number of issues beyond inclusive practices; they helped build a sense of community that crossed professional and grade-level lines and aided many more students with special needs.

> "Are you a professional educator?"
>
> "Yes, I am a parent."
>
> **Conversation at working forum**

PARENTS AS PARTNERS

All of the schools participating in the working forum said that it is essential to consider parents as partners in the school community. Inclusive schools view parents as part of the educational process and often have them as members of their problem-solving teams.

Parents, after all, are their children's first teachers and have a wealth of information that should not be ignored. Besides, it is parents who can make the idea of a school community a reality. When fully engaged, they volunteer in classrooms or at evening and weekend events and are the bridges between home and school communities.

Some schools have included parents in their staff training. Others have made sure that parents were informed of the steps taken toward becoming more inclusive.

Keeping parents informed has sometimes meant that educators must listen to the fears of parents that their children's education would be harmed by more inclusive policies. Parents of children without disabilities often worry that their children's progress will be slowed by being in the same school with children with disabilities. Parents of children with disabilities often worry that their children will flounder in general school settings. Participants in the working forum argued that those fears need to be answered, not by soothing words but by concrete realities. Providing information to the parents and addressing their concerns is all part of parent/teacher interaction.

TEACHERS AS PARTNERS

All of the schools that participated in the conference have been implementing some form of co-teaching. Co-teaching occurs when a special education teacher and a general education teacher team together to instruct a class.

Traditionally, teachers work in isolation from each other, each teacher confined to his or her classroom. Co-teaching requires teachers to give up some of that exclusivity in exchange for gaining a partner to share planning, teaching, discipline, and assessment. As a result, schools using co-teaching become more collegial and cooperative.

One high school math teacher with 25 years of experience reported that before beginning co-teaching, he would never have stopped by another classroom during his preparation period—"It was unheard of." Now, he says, he will often stop by and help a fellow teacher instruct a class and pick up some new techniques for himself. Co-teaching, he says, "gets us away from that goofy isolation."

PARAPROFESSIONALS AS PARTNERS

In every school the paraprofessionals were a quiet key to success. They are both the continuity and support for students, staff, and families. As active participants of the team and school community, they are a critical element to both the planning and delivery of appropriate services to students. In many cases, paraprofessionals are a link to making inclusive schools work.

STUDENTS AS PROBLEM SOLVERS

Students also need to be included in the partnerships and collegial relationships of the school community. Some ways to do this are:

Peer mediation. Peer mediation is a rather formal procedure in which students trained in mediation help resolve disputes among other students.

Student mediators are not asked to handle serious problems involving drugs or weapons, but rather more everyday disputes. "He got me into trouble by copying from my test" might be a dispute handled by peer mediators.

This procedure was not adopted by the schools to build a sense of community but rather to solve a particular problem. However, a side benefit is that students are contributing to the school community to a much greater degree than in the past.

Peer tutoring. Students who help other students learn and review material not only gain the educational benefits of helping teach, but often gain the friendships of other students.

Cross-age tutoring. When older students help younger students learn, they bring a valuable sense of community to the whole school. One high school that participated in the working forum acknowledged juniors and seniors for tutoring students with disabilities by posting photographs of the students working together throughout the school building to provide examples of a community in development.

Cooperative learning. Students within classrooms team up in cooperative learning groups not only to learn new material but also to develop a sense of connection and commonality.

Buddy systems. Buddy systems can be very effective with students of all ages. When the parents of a child with multiple disabilities requested that their child be included in the general classroom, the school paired the child with a friend from the special program. Together the "buddies" went into a general classroom for part of the day with the special education teacher. By pairing the children together, each had a friend with whom to face the strangeness of the new classroom. The teacher reported that each became full members of the class much more quickly than the school staff had expected.

A more usual form of the buddy system is to pair a child with a disability with a child without a disability. Sometimes the pairing is changed daily, sometimes weekly, sometimes less frequently. The child with the disability gets a buddy who helps him function better in the cafeteria, on the playground, and so forth. The child without a disability gains experience in teaching someone else—a powerful learning aid. And, if all goes well, they each gain a friend.

Being someone's buddy can be a very inspiring experience. The mother of a child with a disability told other members of the working forum that the father of her son's buddy told her that some days the major factor that made his son go to school was his responsibility to his buddy.

COMMUNITY MEMBERS AS VOLUNTEERS

Many schools have been working to increase community involvement in schools by requesting that homemakers, retirees, business people, and professionals "mentor" students. The schools also encourage community organizations to do what they can. One school in an urban school district that participated in the working forum has been working with the 4-H, an organization usually associated with rural areas. Among other things, the 4-H organization provided chicken and duck eggs to the school and incubators for hatching them.

The constant flow of people in and out of the schools lets children know that school is an enterprise that the community-at-large takes very seriously. It is a powerful message. It is important to prepare volunteers and coordinate their activities carefully so that they can make meaningful contributions. To do that requires staff time and attention.

> One thing I have found with all the programs that address the needs of children with disabilities is the use of labels, which are then turned into nebulous acronyms. Several times I have listened while professionals threw out their labels and acronyms feeling somewhat alienated until I summoned the courage to ask, "What is...?" Finally yesterday somebody was again talking about "EDBD kids," to which someone responded, "What is an EDBD kid?" which prompted the response from the director of special services in New Jersey, "A very small child."
>
> **Nancy Russo, Moss Elementary School, Metuchen, NJ, about the working forum**

REDUCING THE USE OF JARGON

One of the barriers to creating a sense of community in schools is the use of specialized terms and acronyms that parents, community members, and even many teachers and paraprofessionals do not understand. Although it may sometimes be necessary for professionals to use special terminologies, they should keep this to a minimum and always be ready to explain what they mean in simple terms.

TIME FOR PLANNING

All participants in the working forum agreed that teaching many different kinds of children requires a great deal of planning on the part of teachers. Teachers need to think about how to modify the curriculum for each child; they need to gather materials for hands-on activities; and they

need to collaborate with other staff members on meeting the needs of their students. To achieve all of this, teachers need planning time, and time to speak with the counselor, the special education teacher, the history teacher, and so forth. When the only opportunity to collaborate is during lunch hours or before or after school, collaboration and the quality of instruction suffer. When staff members such as speech therapists are only in the building part of the day or week, collaboration becomes even more difficult.

For these reasons, the schools that participated in the working forum carefully prepared common planning times for teachers and other staff members. Some principals feel so strongly about this issue that they themselves teach classes to give their teachers time to plan together.

Common planning times help break down isolation in schools by permitting more collegiality and cooperation, more sharing of ideas, and mutual inspiration. Although common planning times are arranged for specific educational purposes, the side benefit once more is developing the "sharing, participation, and fellowship" that is the key to a sense of community.

Bringing Services to the Student

Many teachers have complained of the fragmentation of instruction so common in schools today. Just as the teacher interests the class in a science lesson or a story, the speech therapist comes by and pulls Josh out, or the Chapter I aide will pull Adrian out, or the reading specialist will pull Sally out. Not only does this mean Josh, Adrian, and Sally will miss that particular lesson and will need help to catch up, but the constant pullouts also reduce the cohesion of the class.

In many of the schools participating in the working forum, education specialists, related services professionals, and paraprofessionals come to the classroom and work with individuals or groups of students. The resource teacher visits the class during reading group time and works with a small group of students on their reading; the paraprofessional works in the classroom with individual students on math skills; and the speech therapist or occupational therapist work with a group of students.

When pull-out services are needed, effective planning among teachers and related service professionals can prevent fragmentation. Students can obtain the specialized services they need at a mutually agreed upon time that does not interfere with classroom instruction.

Flexible Scheduling

One of the issues facing all schools is how to manage instructional time in the most efficient way possible, not only to teach the curriculum but also to build a sense of community. Strategies offered at the forum follow:

To include family, classmates, and child, we use a communication book for James, an 8-year-old child who is nonverbal. Mother writes in the book and sends pictures. The whole class can read the book, as it is left on James's desk. The children write in the book telling what they have done with James during the day. The book goes home with James. The whole class feels included in what James does at home, and the mother knows some of the activities that James and his classmates do.

Betty Wallace,
Kilmer Elementary School,
Coquitlam, Canada

Separate academic and activity schedules. One middle school has two schedules—an academic schedule and an "activity" schedule covering a wide array of crafts, music, sports, and arts. The activity classes are grouped according to the students' interests and change every 9 weeks. Thus, students who are grouped homogeneously for certain academic classes have the opportunity to interact with other students in nonacademic activities.

Teaching-learning teams. Two participating middle schools gave examples of how they structured small groups of teachers to facilitate greater cohesiveness. These schools divided each of their grades into teams of about 120 students with 5 teachers per team. In some schools, teams stayed together as the students progressed through school. In others, students were part of a different team each year.

Although students take some classes apart from their teams (e.g., foreign languages), they mostly stay within the team structure. Some classes may be grouped according to achievement, but the teams themselves are heterogeneously grouped. In some schools, the students are further grouped into heterogeneous "home bases" or "homerooms" of 15 or more students. To obtain such small groups, almost every educational professional in the building has a home base class including, for example, the librarian and the counselor. The home bases are where students learn study skills or discuss school-wide issues and polices. Through the home-base structure, students with disabilities can attend assemblies and participate in other school-wide activities with students without disabilities. Sometimes, students are permitted to "sign out" of home base and go to the library or other common

rooms. Teachers at these schools know that when a student with a developmental disability or with an emotional difficulty goes to the library with buddies from his home base, then they have succeeded in creating a true community spirit.

In addition to their planning time, teachers meet as a team every day or every other day to discuss thematic approaches or overall teaching strategies. They often plan appropriate team activities such as bowling to develop a sense of community among the team members.

Individual problems often emerge during team planning meetings. Conversations occur such as, "Bobby had a hard time in math class today." "Yeah, he was acting up in science, too. I'll give his parents a call and see what is going on." If it is discovered that Bobby's family is in some kind of crisis, all of his teachers are quickly informed and can provide necessary support to the child. Thus, students, teachers, and parents are connected by consistent and regular communication and no student "gets lost in the system." Parents who wish to find out how their child is doing or who want to express a particular concern to the teachers may attend the team meetings, and thus do not need to seek out individual teachers. If parents

and teachers feel it is necessary, a student can carry a notebook to classes that contains messages from teachers to parents and parents to teachers.

A side benefit of team meetings is that the school teams operate free from the paperwork that many teachers face. If members want to alert a team member about a possible problem with a particular student, a note is made in the team notebook that all team members review daily. These notes are used to alert each other about potential problems that need to be followed, but an initial inquiry does not require massive amounts of paperwork.

In the middle schools that participated in the working forum, every team included a special education teacher who works with the general teachers, making sure each student is appropriately accommodated within the curriculum. Special education teachers may work, for example, with general teachers to enlarge the print for tests for students with visual disabilities or find a "Books for the Blind" tape for a student who learns better aurally than visually. Teachers might discuss a particular student's disability or learning problem and suggest strategies the general or special education teacher might use.

The special education teachers also co-teach in classrooms where there are other students with special needs, providing extra support to explain and modify the curriculum. In heterogeneously grouped classes, teachers assess the capabilities of each student and require differing levels of achievement, but all students are taught from the same basic curriculum and are exposed to the same information and materials. For example, one student learning about Japan in social studies might be required to write a three-page essay while another student is required to write a poem or work with a classmate in a cooperative project about the topic. The fact that all the students are studying Japan, however, means that students feel a greater sense of cohesion and community, and no one feels excluded.

Longer classes. Some secondary schools are experimenting with block scheduling in which students take fewer classes each semester but each class period is longer. This means teachers have fewer students for longer periods, allowing them to keep better track of students and get to know them better, thus adding to the cohesion and sense of community.

Taking a break from the normal schedule. One secondary school has a mid-year "winter term" where special, intensive classes are grouped by interest rather than ability level for 3 weeks. Various community and independent projects are undertaken during this time by students with and without disabilities working together.

Homerooms. One secondary school schedules a ½ an hour between first and second period for "student pursuit time." During this interval, stu-

TEN WAYS TO BUILD A SENSE OF COMMUNITY IN YOUR SCHOOL:

1. Clearly state the goals of the school.
2. Make sure all members of the school community are treated with respect and consideration and that all special efforts are recognized.
3. Invite all staff members and parents to at least some of the teacher training workshops.
4. Hold a few all-school events every year, and make sure everyone feels welcome.
5. Make sure that students have meaningful ways to contribute to the community as tutors, buddies, crossing guards, student council members, peer mediators, and volunteers.
6. Make sure that all the adults in the school can participate in making decisions about the way they do their jobs. For example, teachers should be able to decide what materials best suit their teaching style, and building maintenance workers should be able to decide on the equipment they use and the schedules they follow.
7. Invite professionals and retired professionals in the general community to help in classrooms and with student activities.
8. Make sure parents know what is going on in the classrooms through newsletters, conferences, back-to-school nights, and presentations at PTA and PTSA meetings.
9. Establish systems to encourage collegiality, cooperation, and trust among staff members. Such systems include management teams, co-teaching opportunities, and shared planning times.
10. Use language that everyone can understand when talking about disabilities, class structure, professional services, or any other aspect of what is going on in the school.

Judith Snow had challenges but was raised by her parents at home. However, when they died Judith was placed in an institution. Due to lack of care, Judith became very ill and almost died. Someone who knew of Judith and what was happening called Marsha Forrest. Marsha was involved with "integration" in the Toronto area. Although Marsha didn't know Judith, she called up about 17 of her friends and they gave Judith the round-the-clock care that she needed until she was well and in a better living situation. Out of that concern came the idea of "circles of friends"—support circles for people with disabilities.

These same people also lobbied and changed the law in Canada. Now money can be given to people trying to live a more independent life outside of a government institution. Marsha and Judith have remained very close friends.

Brenda Kearns, Kilmer Elementary School, Coquitlam, Canada

dents consult with teachers and each other. Once a week, students gather in a classroom for a "closed" student pursuit time, and students of different ability levels meet with one teacher to discuss school-wide issues or work on such issues as study skills. This is an opportunity for students who might not ordinarily see each other during the school day to interact and cooperate together on specific skills or subjects.

OTHER OPPORTUNITIES FOR INTERACTION

Many other possibilities exist to make schools into cohesive communities where people know each other and feel a connection. Two ideas contributed by participants in the working forum follow:

Circle of friends. Several schools have instituted a "circle of friends" program in which special education teachers invite students with and without disabilities to go bowling, hiking, or participate in some activity they all can enjoy.

Popcorn. One high school began with a self-contained program for students with profound learning disabilities that was almost completely isolated from the rest of the school. Special education teachers deliberately began eating lunch with the general education teachers to help create the feeling of a cohesive faculty. The teachers assigned the job of managing the supplies needed for shop class to their special education students. Students from the general program who were taking shop had to ask these students for what they needed. Students from the special program were also given other jobs within the school such as

cleaning the teachers' lounges and the cafeteria, which ensured exposure and interaction with the larger school community.

Perhaps the most significant innovation, however, was beginning a small popcorn business. Students in the special program sold popcorn during breaks and gave teachers coupons for free popcorn. This activity brought many teachers and students into the special program classroom. All of these activities worked toward creating a more cohesive school community.

Collaboration, Collegiality, and Partnership

CHAPTER 3

Collaboration, Collegiality, and Partnership

An inclusive school encourages students and staff to support one another and to use all available resources to serve the needs of individual students, resources that include parents and a wide array of community services. In this chapter, some of the educational strategies used to promote collaboration, collegiality, and partnership will be described.

CO-TEACHING

All of the schools that participated in the working forum are trying some form of co-teaching. As previously indicated, co-teaching is when a special education teacher and a general teacher team together to instruct a class. The class is sometimes bigger than a normal-sized single class, but smaller than two classes combined. Teachers report that they can tell when the partnership is working when they stop referring to "my kids" and "your kids" but instead say, "our kids."

All teaching partnerships require collaboration, compromise, and extensive communication. Many co-teachers refer to their partnerships as "marriages," implying a complicated nexus of issues and emotions. The teachers who participated in the forum are adamant that co-teaching benefits not only all students but the teachers as well.

General education teachers and special education teachers bring a tremendous amount of knowledge and skills to the task of teaching, and by being paired together, they pool their expertise. "When you put two teachers together, you get more than double," says one co-teacher. Generally

> **Labels don't work for teachers anymore, either.**
>
> **Special education teacher at working forum**

speaking, general education teachers have more in-depth knowledge about specific curriculums or subject areas being taught. Special education teachers generally know more about modifying and "breaking down" curriculum and adapting teaching methodologies to meet the needs of individual children. When general and special education teachers instruct students and work together, they have more to offer to all of the students. In addition, as teachers learn from each other, compromise, and resolve disagreements, students see adults doing exactly what they are being asked to do.

One of the benefits of co-teaching is that partners provide each other with evaluation and feedback. While one teacher teaches, the co-teacher can act as an audience, sensing when some students are floundering and in need of further instruction. Thus, "I'm finally getting the kind of moment-by-moment evaluation I can trust, not a written summary once or twice a year," reported one teacher at the working forum.

For teachers to reach the point where they welcome such constant evaluation and feedback, they need to have worked out many of the issues involved in teaching together. Teachers need to have discussed not just their overall philosophies of education and teaching, but also the "little things," such as whether or not students may chat about their assignments, sharpen pencils, and move around the classroom.

"I was convinced that students couldn't learn with the buzz of conversation," said one special education teacher who had become accustomed to a very quiet classroom before she co-taught an

English class. The general education teacher eventually convinced her that conversation about assignments "leads to much richer writing." However, it took the special education teacher some time to adjust to the relative chaos of the general classroom.

One of the many benefits of co-teaching is that when one teacher is absent for whatever reason, the class can still proceed with the co-teacher and a substitute instead of remaining in a "holding pattern," as is often the case with the use of substitute teachers. Teachers did emphasize that a substitute teacher is still needed when a partner is absent, however.

In one elementary school that has used co-teaching for 5 years, one of the co-teachers "is promoted" with the class at the end of the year. Therefore, each year the students have one familiar teacher and one new teacher to help them begin the new term without a great deal of "getting acquainted" time. Although it is sometimes difficult for the teachers to break up partnerships after just 1 year, the continuity has proven very helpful to the students. Teachers who have co-taught then train other teachers in co-teaching methods.

Having two teachers in the classroom makes some teaching methods more effective. For example, hands-on activities such as science experiments—proven to be among the most effective methods of teaching—are much easier to plan and carry out with two teachers in the room.

Cooperative learning groups, which will be discussed in more detail later, are increasingly used in classrooms around the country and can be more successful with co-teaching. When only one teacher facilitates cooperative learning groups, they can sometimes get "bogged down." When

two teachers are circulating and helping the groups of students, much more teaching is accomplished.

Testing can be more flexible with co-teaching. For example, some co-teaching teams permit each student to decide whether to take written or oral tests, based on the student's preferred "learning style." While one teacher administers written tests in one area, the other administers the test orally in another area.

Co-teaching is a tremendous help, as well, in managing discipline problems. If a student is misbehaving, one teacher can devote himself to that problem while the class continues uninterrupted. In this way, behavior problems never become unmanageable. "It's virtually impossible to get away with anything in our class now," says one teacher.

One barrier to co-teaching that teachers repeatedly discussed at the working forum, although they were sometimes embarrassed about its "trivial" nature, was the issue of personal space. Teachers are accustomed to being the "rulers" of their rooms and are notorious for disliking any interference. Sharing rooms can be especially difficult. Some special education teachers referred to the welcome they initially received from their general teacher partner as, "This is my room and this is my desk. You may have the wastebasket." The fact is that teachers carefully organize their rooms to reflect their own teaching styles. Teachers have particular ideas about which activities should take place where, and which supplies belong where. To share that control is difficult.

For special education teachers, who are usually the ones asked to give up their classrooms and work in other teachers' classrooms, the territorial issue can be especially painful. Co-teaching "removed me from my own little room where I could do what I thought was best for my students," said one teacher who said she initially had problems of "ownership."

"But, my students were doing well. I could see growth. I saw they were exposed to things they never would have been exposed to in my self-contained class," remarked this teacher. It was difficult for that teacher to communicate to her co-teacher the problems she had in sharing her authority and her environment, but she overcame those difficulties when she saw the benefits to the children involved.

The issue of territory extends even to the issue of desks. "I know it sounds trivial," said this same teacher, "but I needed a desk so that I could tell students when they're finished with their work that they should put it on 'my' desk." She acquired a small typing table that solved the problem.

If the issue of territoriality is addressed outright, it can usually be overcome, and the partnership can flourish. If ignored, it is likely to be a stumbling block.

One principal at the working forum suggested that the "personal space" of teachers should be removed from the learning space of the classroom altogether, in much the same way that college teachers have offices separate from the neutral territory of classrooms.

ROLE RELEASE

School systems depend upon the expertise of numerous professionals, many of them educated in specific methods. "Role release" refers to the idea that specialists work together, sharing their knowledge and skills.

For example, an occupational therapist who works with a student with a physical disability in an art class teaches the student and the teacher adaptive techniques the student can use in order to paint. A speech therapist might work with several children who have articulation problems in their 2nd-grade classroom. In both examples, the

> One teacher jokingly said, "In our school, you can identify the teachers in the teachers' lounge by their facial expressions. The haggard-looking ones with scowls, mumbling to themselves, are the regular teachers. The group in the corner laughing, talking, and planning together are the collaborative teachers." Actually, this sounds like our school as well.
>
> **Kathryn Snider. Marshalltown, IA**

children are served and their teachers are simultaneously taught to use new skills.

Role release raises a couple of thorny issues illustrated by the remarks of a speech therapist who attended the working forum. She said that she had been accustomed to working on her own and having to work in another teacher's room made her very uncomfortable. It also made some of the classroom teachers uncomfortable, several of whom were very hostile at the idea of her intruding into their classroom. Working collaboratively took some adjustment on her part and on the part of the other teachers. But after 5 years, she reported, all the professionals are working well together—even those who were initially reluctant.

The speech therapist also remarked that one of her fears had been that by training the classroom teachers, she would eventually work herself out of a job. She changed her mind one day while working in an elementary classroom with a class that was doing a project with play dough. She was working specifically with a child who was having trouble articulating the "f" sound. As she and the child formed play dough with forks, she was able to elicit the "f" sound twice from the child. The classroom teacher turned excitedly to her and said, "Oh, I see how you did that; I can do that, too!" The speech therapist realized that the child would benefit greatly from spending all day with a teacher who could help him. And, she said, "If we can show children that the adults can share and learn from each other, then they can learn to share and learn from each other."

Furthermore, she found that her expertise would always be needed to help diagnose and solve new problems. In fact, as she pointed out, she now has more time to work directly with students who really require her expertise.

Improved Learning Through Innovative Instruction

CHAPTER 4

Improved Learning Through Innovative Instruction

Children should not be expected to move in lock step, but rather they should be nurtured along their individual paths to learning. This is essential to an inclusive school.

Inclusive schools incorporate techniques such as cooperative learning, curriculum adaptation, peer-tutoring, direct instruction, reciprocal teaching, social skills training, computer-assisted instruction, study skills training, and mastery learning. Groupings are flexible, and material is presented in concrete, meaningful ways that emphasize participation. Although there is less reliance on programs that pull children out of classrooms, there are still opportunities for children to receive separate instruction if needed.

Inclusive schools give each child an opportunity to reach high levels of achievement, measuring that achievement with new forms of assessment and accountability, such as portfolio and performance-based assessment. School teams within inclusive schools make sure than no student is excluded from participation by a rigid environment or inadequate technology.

Following are some specific ways that inclusive schools make sure that they serve the individual needs of children, rather than expecting children to fit the services offered.

CURRICULUM MODIFICATION

One high school math teacher attending the working forum has been co-teaching for several years. He said that the general math class that he teaches includes several students with mental retardation and learning disabilities. He and his co-teacher became increasingly dissatisfied with the math textbook they were using. Their dissatisfaction intensified after attending a conference with business leaders who detailed the kinds of math

knowledge they need employees to know. Although the students with disabilities had prompted their dissatisfaction with the textbook, the teachers became increasingly aware that none of the students in the class were doing as well as possible.

After deciding that the math textbook was ineffective for teaching the kind of math that students will need as they enter the labor force, the two teachers stopped using the book and developed their own materials. Today their students use the materials the teachers have developed, all dealing with real-life math problems, but still covering the same mathematical principles covered in the discarded textbook. As the students work through the materials, they place their work in binders forming a manual that they will eventually be able to take to work with them.

This is but one example of curriculum modifications that are being made in inclusive school settings, where teachers have the freedom to adapt and create curricula better suited to their students' needs.

INDIVIDUAL INSTRUCTION

Some students learn best in groups; others learn better individually. All students need to be offered the opportunity for each kind of instruction.

Although inclusive schools as a whole prefer to keep students in the classroom as much as possible, they do provide separate pullout programs where necessary. Such instruction is provided because it is the best method to meet the student's instructional needs.

COOPERATIVE LEARNING GROUPS

Teachers organize students of different abilities into groups of three or four and assign them a task such as writing a research paper, solving an applied math problem, or conducting a scientific experiment. Each student has a specific role (recorder, for example) in addition to being responsible to the group as a

whole. Students teach each other and learn to co-operate and negotiate, while teachers move from group to group helping the children solve any problems that emerge. (Cooperative learning groups seem to work best with co-teaching, discussed in Chapter 3.)

PEER TUTORING

Teachers have long known that one of the best ways to learn a subject is to teach it to someone else. Teachers use that principle when setting up peer tutoring systems. For instance, they will assign a 3rd-grade student who has grasped the material being taught to instruct another child who has not grasped it. Sometimes older students are utilized to teach younger ones. Peer tutoring is a helpful technique for all schools, but it is especially useful for schools that want to include more children with disabilities.

Peer tutoring permits some students to benefit by being taught by other students who are themselves very close to the learning process and who

can see stumbling blocks invisible to adults. It also permits other students to benefit by teaching, thereby reinforcing their own learning. The only caveat raised about peer tutoring at the working forum was that teachers need to be careful not to always single out the same students as tutors and others as tutees, but to try and make sure there is a balance. In other words, all students can learn from each other.

NEW FORMS OF STUDENT ASSESSMENT

All school systems are grappling with the issue of assessment. How we measure achievement in meaningful ways is a very difficult issue, and beyond our scope to examine in any detail. However, there are a few issues that strongly affect inclusive schools that were raised at the working forum.

One issue is the need to have a standard report card for all students in a school. If some students

have one kind of report card and students classified as having a disability have another (or none, as in some schools) children with disabilities are unnecessarily identified as being different.

One school that uses a standard report card has a small box to mark if a student is being judged on different standards from most children. If the student, for example, is being graded on how well she met the goals listed in her Individualized Education Program (IEP), then that is noted. Teachers in that school have the option to grade any child on a different standard for one marking period. If, for example, a child had a crisis in his family and was distracted and unable to concentrate, the teacher has the option of making such a notation so that the grades in that marking period do not count against the child.

Assessment raises several other issues that must be addressed by schools with inclusive policies. For example, two students may get the same score on a test that do not reflect the same level of effort. For a student with severe learning problems the score may indicate an outstanding performance, while the same score for a student with no disability may reflect a mediocre performance. What grade should each receive? How might each student's performance be better reflected?

Another example: Should the student with learning problems who is getting "A"s by working hard and achieving all the goals on his IEP be on the honor roll?

Not all the schools that participated in the working forum have fully resolved these issues. But one school that includes a substantial number of students with disabilities has 60% of its student body on the honor roll, some of whom are being graded using different standards from the general school population. In that school, the principal says that having the different standards is working very well.

Many of the schools participating in the working forum are using new forms of assessment. Although most still use some form of standardized testing, they are also using alternative assessments, such as portfolio assessment, observation of student performance (e.g., using a science experiment, demonstration, or model), and curriculum-based assessment.

Many of these "new" forms of assessment are not entirely new—teachers have been using them as classroom activities for years! What is novel about them is how they are used—as assessments, they are tied more closely to the curriculum and they are graded using objective scoring criteria. They have the advantage of providing teachers with a different view of what students know; they also allow the students to use a different mode of expression for what they know. These assessments can be embedded in classroom instruction—thereby avoiding student testing fears—and making the assessment closer to instruction; they can be administered in learning groups and can also cut across subject areas, assessing student knowledge in several subjects at the same time.

Like traditional forms of assessment, accommodations for students with disabilities can be made in alternative assessments. Students can be given extra time, can use different media for either questions or responses or both (e.g., audio cassettes), can work in a separate location, or can use other accommodations as appropriate to individual needs. In some cases, alternate forms of the assessments are needed.

The working forum participants were concerned that until colleges and universities agree to review the new forms of assessment in the college entrance process, there will be resistance to them, especially among high school students and their parents.

Another difficulty arises with district and state-wide testing—standardized and performance-based tests designed to gauge how well students have mastered the curriculum. These tests are increasingly used as part of educational reform efforts and, in some locations, are a requirement for high school graduation. At issue is the question whether or not students with disabilities have to pass the test, with or without modification, in order to graduate from high school.

New Jersey educators have wrestled with this question. The state recently instituted what one participant in the working forum called a "very rigorous" test that must be passed in order to graduate from high school. Although students are required to take the test, some students identified as having substantial disabilities may obtain waivers. A waiver permits the student to receive a diploma if he or she achieves certain goals based on his or her IEP. Using this method, as the New Jersey director of special education reported to the working forum, the state balanced the two objectives of high standards and flexible assessments.

Many states allow accommodations as they are described on the student's IEP. The IEP provides a guide to the accommodations that are appropriate and allowable and also ensures that the methods that have been used to instruct the student are the methods used to test the student.

SCHOOL EVALUATION

Not only do students need to be assessed, but also the schools that serve them. It is especially important for any school trying something new to monitor, evaluate, and document what goes on.

Schools moving toward becoming more inclusive should begin by gathering baseline data to present a good picture of the current school functioning. Such data might be test scores; any other measures of achievement; parent, student, and teacher surveys; and other pertinent information.

Many of the participants in the working forum reported that their schools are better by almost all measures than they were before they instituted more inclusive policies. However, only a few participants were able to document their successes with data because most had failed to record the "before" or base-line information. Ongoing data can help school teams do "mid-course" corrections based on feedback regarding the impact of the inclusive school strategies implemented.

NEW TECHNOLOGY

Tremendous advances in technology, both adaptive and instructional, are enabling students with disabilities to learn and be participants in the school community. Today, technology affords students with disabilities opportunities for mobility, communication, self-help, reading, writing, and knowledge acquisition never before envisioned. For example, communication devices that allow nonverbal students to speak have provided students the opportunity to communicate and thereby participate and benefit from more learning environments. The schools that participated in the working forum are finding that technology is a major ingredient in their schools.

A few examples of the high and low technology used in schools follow:

- Tape recordings of lessons for those students who find it difficult or impossible to take notes.
- Taped books for students with visual impairments or learning disabilities who find it difficult to profit from written material.
- Closed captioning for students who are deaf or who have auditory learning disabilities that make it difficult for them to comprehend spoken material.
- Computer software that converts printed text into Braille or voice transmissions, or that speaks the text using a computer equipped with a sound system.

- Computers that permit students who have difficulty forming letters to write and take notes and help those students with learning disabilities correct spelling and grammar.
- Computers that have expanded keyboards or are switch- or voice-activated for students who cannot move their hands.
- Computers that speak for students with visual impairments.
- Photocopiers and computer printers that enlarge text for students with visual impairments.
- "Surroundsound" stereo-listening devices for students who are hard of hearing.
- Computer networks that permit students and teachers to access information and communicate with others outside the school, thereby expanding the school community and resource options.
- Computer software that enables professionals to assess a student's mastery of the curriculum and design appropriate instruction and curricular modifications.
- Computer software that permits students, individually or in groups, to master curricular goals by using computer programs that make maximum use of the students' learning styles and abilities, monitor progress, and provide for interaction with the teacher.
- Video disc, virtual reality, and other emerging technologies that empower students to learn from and explore the universe, regardless of their disability.

Technology is a powerful tool for achieving educational opportunity for all students in an inclusive school. Participants at the working forum reported that the more they learned about technology and experienced its potential, the more they realized the need for additional technology, including training about how to use it, classroom environments to accommodate it, and connections with the home and community.

ACCESS

School buildings need to be designed properly in order to be inclusive. Physical barriers should be removed for children with disabilities. This has been, and will remain for some time, an important issue, especially in older schools with lots of stairs and no elevators. Schools with portable classrooms face additional problems.

Following are two issues related to the availability and use of space that participants at the working forum raised:

Classrooms need to be big enough and class sizes small enough so that teachers are able to use a variety of instructional approaches and students are able to navigate easily. For example, rooms should not be completely filled with desks and chairs, thus blocking the way for children in wheelchairs to go to the blackboard. Classrooms may also need to be equipped with round tables instead of, or in addition to desks, to facilitate cooperative learning groups, peer tutoring, large and small group instruction, and the technologies and materials needed by all the students. As one teacher at the working forum said, "You can't do inclusion at desks."

For those children with emotional and behavioral problems and other students who may need it, schools must have effective behavioral management strategies in place including safe, supervised areas (other than the principal's office or another classroom) where children can retreat or be sent to regroup before returning to the classroom. Without that safety valve, behavioral problems become very difficult to manage. One special education resource teacher who participated in the working forum complained that her room had become the time-out room. The unscheduled arrival of a student having a tantrum or other emotional outburst was just as disruptive to the students she was working with individually, or in small groups, as it was to the teacher who sent the student.

Leadership in an Inclusive School

CHAPTER 5

Leadership in an Inclusive School

A ll schools require strong leadership. But inclusive schools, where developing a common vision and sense of community are so important, require even more skillful and dedicated leadership than most. That leadership should be used to set up the structures and systems within the school that support the classroom teachers and other school professionals.

Following are the types of structures and supports principals and central administrators need to put in place to make an inclusive school successful.

SITE-BASED AUTHORITY

As in almost all schools, the building principal is the key leader in an inclusive school. It is the principal who sets the tone for the school, determining whether schools will be communities of learning or just buildings full of disparate and disconnected activities. It is the principal's responsibility in collaboration with teachers to make sure that all staff members, all students, and all parents, as well as a variety of outside community members, feel a part of the school. It is the principal who must provide for appropriate and ongoing staff training and support required to meet student needs. And, it is the principal who makes sure staff members have the time they need to plan and consult.

Participants in the working forum agreed that principals play a critical and key leadership role. For this reason, many participants argued that schools need to have the authority to make decisions. If principals are required to request permission for every accommodation needed for individual students, administration becomes cumbersome and often impossible.

SHARING LEADERSHIP

One of the most important ways principals provide leadership in an inclusive school is by sharing it, enabling other staff members to identify and solve problems. One tactic effective principals employ is to set up problem-solving teams (discussed in Chapter 2). Although different schools call their teams by different names, all the schools represented at the working forum had some kind of team consisting of the principal, classroom teachers, paraprofessionals, usually a parent, and the other professionals needed—the school psychologist or the school counselor, or related service professionals.

At these problem-solving team meetings, which some schools hold monthly or more often, teams rely on their collective expertise to determine appropriate classroom solutions or specialized services needed to solve specific student needs. Decisions can be made quickly and efficiently when all of the professionals who participate in the decision meet together.

SCHEDULING PLANNING TIME

The expression "time is money" has special meaning for inclusive schools, and finding time sometimes means finding money—another scarce resource.

Following are some methods that enabled teachers to find time to plan and consult:

- One school district increased the schools' instructional time by 3 minutes a day, which permitted them to have 4 "early release" days for teachers to plan and attend training workshops.
- In one school district, the union contract stipulates that a teacher who has a student with substantial disabilities must receive $400 worth of substitute time throughout the year (about 10 half-days), time the teacher uses to plan and collaborate.
- One high school has a "floating sub," a substitute teacher who works only in that school and relieves teachers of classroom duty on a regular schedule of 20 minutes every 6 days.
- In one elementary school where teachers are expected to supervise the children's recess, the principal does so instead, freeing the teachers for planning.

- In several schools, substitute time is used in order that teachers can plan together. Although they appreciate the time, teachers complain that preparing lesson plans for substitutes sometimes takes as much time as the time "freed up." One school found a substitute who developed an art lesson for several grade levels with modifications for students with disabilities. This cut down on the time teachers needed to prepare for substitutes in order to have planning time.
- Stipends can be provided for teachers during the summer and evenings for staff development or planning.
- Schools can hire additional teachers to rotate through the classrooms, permitting teachers to plan or even to share classes.

Working forum participants recommended that educators spend as little time as possible on "administrivia" so that they can serve the needs of the students rather than the institution. Some suggestions include:

- Administrative matters can be handled by memoranda or bulletin boards, allowing faculty meetings to be used for professional development and school-wide planning.

- A regularly scheduled staff development newsletter or "read and pass" folders can provide information to staff regarding inclusive school strategies.
- Schools equipped with computers can use E-mail to facilitate communication and sharing among staff members.

STAFF DEVELOPMENT

All schools need to provide staff members with regular, ongoing training and education that is delivered in a manner that models the practice that is being taught. Staff development is an especially crucial issue when schools include students with disabilities. Teachers, paraprofessionals, and substitute teachers all need specific training in what disabilities their students have, what kinds of teaching techniques are best suited for those students, and how technology can be useful. They also need to keep abreast of the latest thinking in their subject areas and share notes on how to best teach specific lessons.

In addition, all adults in the school need to know what to expect from students with disabilities and how they can encourage them to achieve. If a school has a child with cerebral palsy, for example, all staff need to know what supports are needed for the student; the food service workers need to know whether to help the child with his food tray or encourage him to carry it himself; and when the child is late to school, the school secretary needs to know whether to sign him in or ask him to sign himself in. These issues can be crucial to the child's sense of accomplishment and responsibility, and they require the training and collaboration of all staff members.

Several participants in the working forum expressed frustration that the type and extent of staff development is often determined by central administrators rather than by the school staff. They said that teachers and other school staff should be able to design their own learning opportunities so that they can learn additional skills and acquire information more directly related to the learning needs of their students.

REDEPLOYING RESOURCES

Many schools are organized into separate structures that serve important needs, but they often

> **Educators know that "creating" new time is impossible, but "finding" time is vital.**
>
> **Diane Rae, Capital High School, Olympia, WA**

do so in isolation from each other. Classrooms are separate; support services such as speech therapy, psychological testing, Chapter 1 services (federal assistance to low-income and at-risk students), and so forth, often operate autonomously out of sight of the rest of the school. These barriers must be broken for schools to become more inclusive. In so doing, schools will be better suited to serve the needs of all students.

Participants at the working forum indicated that it was important to think of special education not as a place but as a service. It should be perceived as a set of supports and services to meet individual students' needs.

When considered in that context, it is easy to think "inclusively," participants said. That is, if a child needs life skills education, what is the best way to provide curriculum and/or instructional strategies that can effectively teach it? Perhaps the child would be best served in a special education room or perhaps the child would derive greater benefits from being in a general classroom with the services brought to the student. By working collaboratively, educators and parents should have the freedom to determine and provide what is best for the students.

The schools that participated in the working forum used a number of strategies to include students in general classrooms. The most common are:

- *Co-teaching.*
- *Reducing class size* to make it easier to provide necessary support to diverse learners. For example, if a typical class contains 28 students, a class should contain only 26 students if one is a student with substantial disabilities. That student could also be assigned a full- or part-time paraprofessional. Participants in the conference seemed to agree that no class with only one teacher should have more than three students who need a great number of special education services.
- *Assigning paraprofessionals to students with disabilities.* Many inclusive schools use paraprofessionals to help students with disabilities. For students with physical disabilities, the paraprofessionals help overcome physical obstacles in the classroom. For those with learning disabilities, the paraprofessionals help them to master and review material. For

those with emotional disabilities, paraprofessionals can help manage behavior and contain disruptions.

Forum participants noted that although paraprofessionals may concentrate on overcoming the problems of one student, they also work, as much as possible, with the whole class. In this way, the child with disabilities feels less singled out and the other children gain an additional active adult helping them. In some school districts, this extension of services is expressly forbidden by state administrative and/or funding policy. Conference participants urged that federal and state rules expressly allow paraprofessionals, funded with federal or state special education resources, when appropriate, to provide incidental benefits to other students.

Many of the participants at the working forum stated that paraprofessionals are crucial to successful inclusive schools. For that reason, they said, it is important to include paraprofessionals as full members of problem-solving teams in training workshops and as participants during common planning times. Conference participants also stated that the success of inclusive schools is jeopardized when paraprofessionals are not treated appropriately.

- *Bring related services to classrooms.* Many of the schools participating in the working forum incorporate support services into the classrooms when appropriate. Speech therapists, occupational and physical therapists, and psychologists, for example, participate in classroom activities.

The participants in the working forum agreed that inclusive schools are not a less expensive way of meeting the educational needs of students, at least in the "short run." To provide the staffing, environment, technology, planning time, and staff development required by an inclusive school takes significant resources. While the participating schools argued that the current levels of funding for education made their efforts challenging, they were able to find creative ways to obtain resources. For example, funds previously spent on transporting students to other schools in the district, or out of the district could be spent on adaptive technology, curricular adaptation, purchase of specialized therapy within the general school, and so on.

One school originally housed three separate programs under one roof—a preschool program for children with disabilities, a program for elementary school students who were deaf or hard of hearing, and a general kindergarten through 8th-grade program. Each ran its own busing system.

When the principal combined the bus services, she was able to use the money saved for other needs.

Another school that had traditionally placed a number of students in private schools was able to use the money that would have been used for their tuition to serve the students in their school.

In another school, school psychologists no longer spend excessive time testing students, but rather spend more time working with teachers, parents, and children, thereby adding an additional support resource to the classroom.

Participants in the working forum agreed that resources should follow the child rather than the child following or being sent to the program. That is, resources should be allocated to meet student needs regardless of where they are served, rather than making decisions about where to serve students based on the location of resources.

I was surprised that one of the schools that participated in the working forum did not work with the union when trying to build the model for inclusion. I feel that if you can work with the union membership to build your model you will have a better chance of teacher backing for the program.

Harry Scott.
Dorseyville Middle School.
Pittsburgh. PA

A barrier to creating more inclusive schools is that certain kinds of services can no longer be provided in the most cost-effective way. For example, if students with certain disabilities are all in one special school, that school will have a large enough population to support a full-time medical staff, full-time occupational and physical therapists, and so on. When students with disabilities attend their neighborhood school instead, it means that schools with few students with disabilities will still need high-cost medical and therapeutic services. Some inclusive schools find that it is very difficult to have, for example, a speech therapist for only 1 or 2 half days because communication and consultation becomes very difficult. Schools implementing inclusive school practices are continuing to explore creative and effective ways to provide needed support for individual children with disabilities.

How We Can All Work to Create More Inclusive Schools

CHAPTER 6

How We Can All Work to Create More Inclusive Schools

WHAT STATE AND LOCAL SCHOOL BOARD MEMBERS AND CENTRAL ADMINISTRATORS CAN DO TO SUPPORT INCLUSIVE SCHOOLS:

1. Make sure that funding follows the students so that schools can make placement decisions based on the needs of the student rather than the location of the money. That way, schools can hire the necessary people and obtain the resources they require to serve the child.

2. Provide time and money for continuing professional development of teachers, administrators, related services professionals, paraprofessionals, and support service workers in the school. Let the school staffs plan the type and extent of professional development to be offered; at a minimum it should include:
   a. information on specific conditions and disabilities. If a school has a child who is blind, for example, everyone who works in the building should know what to expect and what to ask of the child.
   b. specific information on how to manage discipline problems and how to encourage good behavior and a good attitude toward learning. All personnel in the building should have this training.
   c. specific information on how to accommodate different learning styles and how to encourage learning in all children. Teachers and paraprofessionals need to know what special needs their students have and how to meet them, working collaboratively with other professionals and parents.

3. Provide incentive grants to schools to develop their own inclusive policies and practices.

4. Build in planning time for teachers, related service professionals and paraprofessionals during the school year so that they can plan not only individually but as grades and teams.
   Few school districts have addressed the need of paraprofessionals to be included in planning. Many paraprofessionals meet together on their own time, but rarely meet with teachers. For inclusive schools to work properly, teachers and paraprofessionals need time to confer and plan together.

5. When building new schools, make sure buildings are fully accessible to individuals with disabilities and accommodate an inclusive program. Assess existing buildings for necessary changes to make them fully accessible.

6. Use Individualized Education Programs (IEPs) as long-range planning tools with short-term strategies so that all students with disabilities graduate with as much confidence and ability to function in the world as possible. Consider the use of IEPs for all students.

7. Support the development of new assessment methods. Portfolios and curriculum-based assessments should play a larger role, standardized tests a smaller one.

8. When hiring new professionals, seek candidates with collaborative skills, knowledge of disabilities, and a desire to work in inclusive schools.

9. Permit principals and school-based teams to make decisions about scheduling, staffing, curriculum, and materials.

10. Remember that paraprofessionals are integral to the success of inclusive schools.

11. Make sure that paraprofessionals assigned to specific children with disabilities are not precluded from providing incidental benefits to other children.
12. Give foreign language credit to courses in sign language.
13. Remember that inclusive schools are not another way of saying placement in the "least expensive environment."
14. Maintain access to the full continuum of services and settings. While inclusive schools serve the needs of many students, there will be some children who will need special education and related services in other environments.
15. Involve associations, unions, and other pertinent groups in the planning and implementation of inclusive school practices.

WHAT ASSOCIATIONS AND UNIONS CAN DO TO SUPPORT INCLUSIVE SCHOOLS:

1. Participate in district-wide and school-based planning.
2. Develop policies to support the development and implementation of effective inclusive schools.
3. Assure that members have the appropriate working conditions and resources to assure good practice in an inclusive school.
4. Monitor the progress of inclusive schools and provide feedback to members, school officials, and the public.
5. Assist schools to obtain the resources necessary to run an effective inclusive school.
6. Counsel and assist members in developing new roles for themselves to maximize their value in an inclusive school.
7. Help model and create environments that facilitate collaborative working relationships among school personnel and parents.
8. Provide professional development to members to improve their knowledge and skills in working with students with disabilities and research practices that will improve the delivery of quality instruction.

WHAT PRINCIPALS CAN DO TO SUPPORT INCLUSIVE SCHOOLS:

1. Organize a team of parents and staff members, including yourself, to help plan inclusive school strategies and practices.
2. Make sure teachers, paraprofessionals, substitute teachers, related services personnel, other building support staff, and parents get the ongoing training and support they need.
3. Make sure teachers and paraprofessionals get the planning time they need.
4. Arrange visits for teachers and other staff to inclusive schools.
5. Explore co-teaching with your staff and ask for volunteers. Teachers who are forced into co-teaching may resent it and fail before they even start. Begin with one classroom where success is likely and work from there. Success will stimulate emulation.
6. Know the rights of students with disabilities and their families and the responsibilities of school personnel. Be sure that the inclusive school efforts are consistent with those rights and responsibilities.
7. Use the same report card for all students. Don't single out some students with separate report cards. If a child is being assessed by different criteria from the other children, this can be noted on the standard form.
8. Make sure parents are full partners in your school. Parents are the first teachers children have and commonly have an enormous store of knowledge about their children. They are often the key to creating a sense of community.
9. Have a clear, understandable policy on discipline so that every child and every adult in the school knows what is expected. This policy is especially important for children with behavioral and emotional problems and the adults who care for them.
10. Establish a school-wide behavior management plan so that the staff can be assured that support will be provided at critical times. Because of the additional and often unpredictable nature of supports needed for students with emotional and behavioral difficulties, a school or district-wide behavior management plan should be developed to support teachers working in inclusive schools.

11. Make sure that the focus is always on what each child needs. Some children may need to be away from the distractions of general classrooms for part or all of the day. Provide a variety of settings and options as determined by student needs and staff.

12. Provide teachers with a list of resources including the phone numbers of specialists inside and outside the school system.

13. Monitor and assess constantly. Begin with baseline data and gather information from a number of sources, including observation, test scores, and parent, student, and teacher surveys. Use evaluation information to inform and direct changes in inclusive school practices.

14. Engage the outside community to work in the school. Retirees and local businesses are resources that can be used to connect students with the outside world.

15. Remember that not everything will work. Be willing to fail, regroup, and try a different approach. Let your staff know that failure is something to be learned from, not something to be punished for.

16. Empower and support your staff. It takes all of your combined talent to be an inclusive school.

WHAT TEACHERS CAN DO TO SUPPORT INCLUSIVE SCHOOLS:

1. Be open to the possibility of including a student with disabilities in your classroom.

2. Seek the proper information, professional development, and support. If you are teaching a child with a disability, make sure you know about the child's limitations and potential and about available curriculum methodologies and technology to help the child learn. Insist that any needed services be provided and that the paraprofessional working in your room also get the proper training. If the school is resistant, and the district unresponsive, work with your teacher union or association to get the support you need.

3. Use a buddy system. Pair children with disabilities with children who can help. Occasionally permit students without disabilities to accompany their buddies to pullout programs to let them see what goes on. This reduces the sense of mystery and difference.

4. Use a variety of teaching strategies. Rely less on the "lecture, question, discussion" method and more on hands-on activities, peer tutoring, cooperative learning, and individualized instruction.

5. With co-teaching:
   - Co-teaching relationships should be voluntary. Choose someone you respect and can work well with. As with any other partnership, you need to work hard to make it succeed.
   - Plan on spending time discussing all the decisions that need to be made in a classroom, from the big philosophical issues to the small ones, such as when students may sharpen their pencils and talk about their assignments. Discuss the territorial issues of where things belong, what activities should take place where, and who controls what desk.
   - Remember the advice of one co-teacher— "If the marriage isn't working, get a divorce." (But you might want to try counseling first!)

WHAT PARAPROFESSIONALS CAN DO TO SUPPORT INCLUSIVE SCHOOLS:

1. Learn as much as possible about the strengths of the children you are assigned to.

2. Concentrate not only on the children with disabilities but work with all the children.

3. Seek the proper training and support you need to manage behavioral problems, encourage success, and accommodate different learning styles.

WHAT SUPPORT SERVICE STAFF CAN DO TO SUPPORT INCLUSIVE SCHOOLS:

1. Make schools welcoming places for all students. Every adult is part of the atmosphere of that school. School secretaries, food service workers, maintenance workers, and bus drivers all help make schools welcoming, comfortable places or forbidding, punishing places.

2. Learn about the students in the school and what to expect of them.

3. Be an active member of the school community.

WHAT RELATED SERVICES STAFF CAN DO TO SUPPORT INCLUSIVE SCHOOLS:

1. Work in classrooms more and in separate environments less.
2. "Role release" by training teachers and paraprofessionals how to do some of the more routine aspects of your job. For example, speech therapists can instruct teachers how to encourage proper articulation. This benefits the children and frees the speech therapists to concentrate on more profound language disabilities. Also, psychologists can work with teachers in identifying different learning styles and modifying the curriculum to accommodate them.
3. Be collaborative. Serve on problem-solving teams and be involved in other planning efforts.
4. Be an active part of the school community.

WHAT PARENTS CAN DO TO SUPPORT INCLUSIVE SCHOOLS:

1. Know your child. You are your child's first teacher, and often know better about what he or she is capable of than anyone else. Communicate your hopes and plans to your child's teacher.
2. Actively participate in your child's school. Parents are part of what make a school a community. Volunteer in the classroom if possible; if not, help organize evening and weekend school-wide activities. Treat all students and other members of the school community with respect.
3. If your child has a disability, explain what the disability is to your child's teacher and what services you think your child needs. Monitor the classroom carefully to see if your child is learning as much as he is able.
4. Be a team player. Everyone working together will create a better school.

WHAT COLLEGES AND UNIVERSITIES CAN DO TO ENCOURAGE INCLUSIVE SCHOOLS:

1. In setting admissions standards, agree to look at student portfolios, rather than only SAT scores and grades.
2. Assure that teacher training programs provide future teachers with the skills to modify curricula and use a variety of teaching strategies to instruct all students. Also, provide student teaching opportunities in inclusive schools.
3. Give foreign language credit for sign language.

I was a 2nd-year teacher, in my 1st year of having a fully-included student. Things were absolutely chaotic, and I had no support. In desperation, I turned to my graduate professor for my mainstreaming class, who was also the director of special education at the college. "I have nowhere else to turn; the mainstreaming class didn't prepare me for this," I told him. "I want to know my rights, if I have any. Tell me why you didn't talk about this during my teacher training." The professor calmly explained that it was because, "No one is doing full inclusion around here."

"I'm living it," I argued, "and you need to begin teaching about it."

**Michele Brynjulson,
Golden View Elementary,
San Ramon, CA**

Participating
Schools

BLOOMINGTON HIGH SCHOOL NORTH
Bloomington, Indiana

Bloomington High School North has 1,350 students in 9th through 12th grades. Bloomington city, with a population of about 53,000, is the county seat and the home of the state's largest university, which has had a long and fruitful partnership with the school. Bloomington North draws from urban, suburban, rural, and university communities. About 110 of Bloomington North's students have disabilities.

Bloomington North has about 80 full- and part-time professionals, including 9 special education teachers, 8 teacher assistants, and 4 professionals providing related services.

Bloomington excludes no students, regardless of the degree of disability, and believes that all students should be taught together. It has moved those students with mild disabilities into general education classrooms, decreasing the number of separate, pull-out classes from 21 self-contained classes in 1989-1990 to 4 in 1993-1994. Special education teachers are paired with classroom teachers to modify and adapt the curriculum and instruction. All students have benefited from the presence of two teachers in class, and students with disabilities have benefited by being exposed to a broader curriculum and higher expectations.

The goal for students with substantial disabilities is that they leave school with the skills necessary to live, work, and play in the community; their curriculum is carefully designed to achieve that end. They spend a considerable amount of time training for jobs and holding jobs. Community training experiences are planned with the involvement of a physical therapist, occupational therapist, and the speech and language teacher. They often attend general education classes with peer tutors—juniors and seniors who receive course credit—and attend athletic and musical events, prom, and graduation.

Two specific programs were developed in the past 3 years as a result of the school-wide restructuring effort. The first is a 3-week period called Winter Intensive Term during which all students with disabilities are fully included in general education classes, and no special education classes are offered. Teacher assistants and peer tutors provide any support necessary for students with substantial disabilities.

The second new program is a 30-minute period during the day called Student Pursuit Time. All staff, including teachers, special education teachers, administrators, and counselors are assigned a heterogeneous group of approximately 22 students. One day a week the group meets in a classroom, and the other 4 days students go to various locations in the building. Convocations and class meetings are held during these periods, and students with disabilities are integrated into these programs with their peers.

Bloomington High School, N., 3901 Kinser Pike, Bloomington, IN 47404.

CAPITAL HIGH SCHOOL
Olympia, Washington

Capital High School has 1,388 students and is the largest of the two high schools in the Olympia School District, a three-city area with a population of 56,000. The district has approximately 8,500 students. About 7%, or 101 students, at Capital High are in the special education program. Olympia, the state capital of Washington State, is about 60 miles south of Seattle.

Capital has about 65 teachers; 6 of whom are special education teachers, 4 are counselors, and 2 are assistant principals. In addition, it has 14 educational assistants, of whom 11 are special education assistants, 9 are secretaries, and 5 are custodians.

Capital High opened in 1976 with the beginning of a philosophy that set the stage for a program that incorporates a large diversity of students into the mainstream of school life.

In 1978, a self-contained program for students with developmental disabilities became a part of Capital High School. Through a process of "reverse mainstreaming," peer tutors were instrumental in introducing these students to high school life and activities.

During this period, support services were introduced for the population with learning disabilities. The resource model for academics was gradually abandoned and support services began to be redefined. These support services took the form of study skills classes for all students, an academic mentor program that was beneficial to everyone involved, and educational assistants that provided support in regular classes. The power to make

these decisions within the building allowed special education teachers the flexibility to redefine their role and provide leadership in this change process.

To make inclusion successful, Capital High developed strategies to prepare and assist all the members of the school community. For special education teachers and regular teachers it provided extra training and more planning time. Meetings were set up between the special education staff and the regular teachers, who were enabled to use the services of a "floating substitute" to cover their classes.

The staff recognized that in order to meet the needs of all students, the vocational component needed to be expanded. An educational assistant was hired to develop jobs and give students experiences to make them ready for work.

A goal was set to provide 18- to 21-year-old students with significant disabilities an environment comparable to that of their nondisabled peers. To accomplish this, the base of operation for this population was moved to a local community college campus.

Capital High School, 2707 Conger Avenue, West, Olympia, WA 98502.

CHURCH LANE ELEMENTARY TECHNOLOGY SCHOOL
Baltimore County, Maryland

Church Lane Elementary has 450 students enrolled in prekindergarten through 5th grades. Church Lane is located in Baltimore County, a diverse and changing community, which surrounds Baltimore city. It includes many cultural and socioeconomic backgrounds. The vision of education in Baltimore County public schools is based on the philosophy that students of all exceptionalities are given every opportunity to learn and become productive adults in our society. Inclusive education for students with disabilities is a major focus of our school system.

In the school systems' efforts to provide for children, principles of inclusion have been established. A continuum of services is available with inclusion as an option. At present, Baltimore County is working in conjunction with the Maryland Coalition for Inclusive Education and the Maryland State Department of Education to create neighborhood inclusive schools for all students. The goal of this joint venture is to establish two model schools to be the basis for increased inclusion throughout the county.

As a result of the leadership of the Office of Special Education, the county support system now includes an inclusion development specialist, an inclusion facilitator, a team of resource speech-language pathologists, and an assistive technology facilitator.

Over the past 10 years, Church Lane has moved from a self-contained intensity IV learning disabilities class within the building to a resource room mode with mainstreaming. In 1991, the faculty began looking at adopting the principles of inclusion by participating in workshops, staff development activities, and site visits. Currently, the general education classes include students with speech/language problems, learning disabilities, serious emotional disturbances, and intellectual, physical, and multiple disabilities.

All Church Lane students are able to use new technology, such as a video lab, an integrated learning system, telecommunications, and interactive distance learning.

Church Lane Elementary, 3820 Fernside Road, Randallstown, MD 21133.

DORSEYVILLE MIDDLE SCHOOL
Pittsburgh, Pennsylvania

Dorseyville Middle School has 935 students attending 6th, 7th, and 8th grades, of which approximately 14% are identified as needing educational support. Dorseyville is part of the Fox Chapel Area School District in a suburban area north of Pittsburgh. The district includes six municipalities representing a wide range of social, economic, cultural, and religious backgrounds.

Dorseyville has 78 professional full-time staff, including 7 educational support teachers. Additional support is provided by 5 paraprofessionals and a shared speech therapist. The district contracts for occupational therapy, physical therapy, as well as vision and hearing specialists.

Students at Dorseyville are grouped in three to six teams at each grade level. On each team are four regular education teachers and one educational support specialist who share a common space, planning time each day, and the responsibility of providing instruction for all students on the team. The teaching team collaboratively plans instruction for all students. Instructional groupings and methods vary depending on the needs of students.

The team approach has benefited all students on the teams. At Dorseyville, a variety of instructional strategies are utilized and promoted, including cooperative learning and mastery learning. In addition, classes are moving toward individualized instruction that allows all students to work on projects at their own pace. New instructional software for computers has increased opportunities for students to work independently.

The Dorseyville staff recognizes the importance of encouraging friendships and social interactions among students. One strategy they use is to generate interest and participation in the established intramural program. The Circle of Friends program is another strategy used to support and encourage the development of friendships between students with disabilities and their peers.

Staff development has been one of the key elements in the success of inclusion at Dorseyville. Initial integration team training was provided through "GATEWAYS: Pennsylvania's Statewide System Project." GATEWAYS staff provided on-site technical assistance.

Dorseyville Middle School, 550 Faxonburg Blvd., Pittsburgh, PA 15238.

GOLDEN VIEW SCHOOL
San Ramon, California

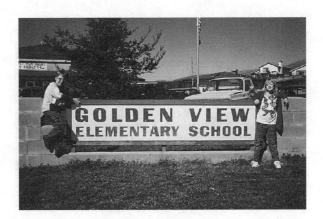

Golden View has 630 students attending kindergarten through 6th grade. Golden View is in the San Ramon Valley Unified School District and serves a suburban area of large single-family homes and some condominiums and apartments.

Golden View has 21 classroom teachers in addition to specialists in science, physical education, instrumental music, and computer education. Golden View is also served by a resource specialist, speech therapist, health educator/nurse, and a full inclusion support teacher.

San Ramon Valley Unified School District has a philosophy that promotes special education as a "part of," not apart from a unified educational system that provides opportunities for all students. To promote this philosophy, the district has adopted a "5-year plan for inclusive education" that provides inclusive opportunities for all special education students. The development of this 5-year plan was accomplished through a task force that included special education teachers, classroom teachers, parents, school board members, paraprofessionals, principals, and administrators.

San Ramon Valley Unified School District's full inclusion program currently serves 17 students with severe disabilities at four neighborhood schools. Golden View is one of those neighborhood schools. San Ramon Valley has assigned two full inclusion specialists to assist teachers, parents, and students to collaborate for successful program implementation. Common planning time is also provided for general education teachers and support staff.

By participating in peer tutoring, cooperative learning, and small group and individual instruction, students with and without disabilities are all benefiting from full inclusion.

Golden View Elementary School, 5025 Canyon Crest Drive, San Ramon, CA 94583.

KILMER ELEMENTARY SCHOOL
Coquitlam, British Columbia

Kilmer Elementary School has 620 students from kindergarten through 7th grade. Kilmer is the largest elementary school in Coquitlam, a suburban area and one of the fastest growing districts in British Columbia. Coquitlam now organizes its schools into K-7th, 8th-10th, and 11th-12th grades, but is reorganizing to develop elementary schools (K-5th grades), middle schools (6th-8th grades), and high schools (9th-12th grades).

Kilmer has two tracks: French immersion, which includes about 45% of the students, and English. About 10% of the students speak English as a second language. The school is becoming more ethnically and culturally diverse, which enhances the philosophy of inclusion at Kilmer.

Kilmer has 35 teachers, including 4 special education teachers and 6 paraprofessionals, including 4 special education paraprofessionals. Support staff includes 2 secretaries, 3 custodians, and 5 lunch and playground supervisors.

Every student is welcomed at Kilmer within its catchment area. It has a long history of providing appropriate education programs for students with special needs. At one time, it housed two self-contained programs, but within the last 3 years has moved to full adoption of the inclusive schools philosophy. Students, previously identified with special needs and pulled out for their special education programs, are now full participating members of their regular classes. Through collaboration, the classroom teacher, parents, support teacher and special education assistant, indi-

vidual student needs and classroom needs are addressed.

The school uses a variety of teaching strategies, including cooperative learning, peer tutoring, peer counseling, peer mediation, mentoring, and team teaching. A new technique currently being implemented is multilevel instruction. Time is provided for both weekly planning team and for collaborative planning team meetings. This planning time is viewed as the cornerstone of the program.

As an inclusive school, Kilmer models a welcoming and accepting attitude, which fosters belonging and brings about a true sense of community.

Kilmer Elementary School, 1575 Knappen Street, Port Coquitlam, BC, Canada V3C 2P8.

LINCOLN MIDDLE SCHOOL
Syracuse, New York

Lincoln has 637 students attending 6th, 7th, and 8th grades, more than half of whom come from outside the attendance area and 68% of whom receive free lunch. Sixteen percent of the students are identified as having disabilities. Lincoln is one of seven middle schools in Syracuse, a city of about 160,000 people in upstate New York.

Lincoln has an administrative staff of one principal, one vice principal, and a dean of students. It has 42 teachers, of whom 8 are special education teachers, and 11 are paraprofessionals. Support staff includes 1 guidance counselor, 1 psychologist, 1 alcohol and drug counselor, 1 part-time social worker, 1 school nurse, 1 librarian, 1 police officer, 3 secretaries, 4 hall monitors, 4 custodial workers, and 6 cafeteria workers.

Although students with disabilities have long been a part of Lincoln, in 1991 Lincoln began planning for its first program to fully include students with disabilities. The plan was triggered by the fact that students with disabilities who had been fully included in elementary school were about to graduate to the middle school. As part of its planning, the Lincoln Inclusive Education Committee had as its goal not only to improve the school for students with disabilities but for all the students.

In 1993 Lincoln adopted a 3-year plan aiming at changing itself from a traditional school focused on separate subjects, facts, and skills taught in isolation to one that aims at integrated, thematic learning using cooperative learning and new as-

sessment methods. The new assessments, including student portfolios, will measure the way students have mastered concepts and skills that often cut across traditional subject areas.

By changing the way it operates, Lincoln feels it is able to concentrate on individual students and how they learn. Its inclusive program is still a "work-in-progress" as staff members continue the effort to develop effective teaching methods for all students.

Lincoln began with a team structure but has since decided that the structure needed considerable changes, including changes in the way students were assigned to teams in order to make the teams more heterogeneous, and changes in scheduling. Each team was to be given the opportunity to devise its own schedule to permit such activities as team lunches, regular team meetings, and block scheduling, allowing some classes to be longer than others.

Lincoln's plan calls for supporting students at different levels. For example, some students might need individual instruction each day, while others might need the presence of a special education teacher or assistant in their classrooms on an ongoing basis.

Lincoln Middle School, 1613 James Street, Syracuse, NY 13203.

MILLER MIDDLE SCHOOL
Marshalltown, Iowa

Miller Middle School has 690 students in 6th, 7th, and 8th grades. Miller is one of two middle schools in Marshalltown, Iowa, a community of approximately 30,000 residents located in central Iowa.

It has the equivalent of 43 full-time teachers, 7-1/2 of whom are special education teachers. In addition, it has 12 paraprofessionals, 8 of whom specialize in special education. About 100 students are identified as needing special education services.

In January 1991, Miller began a building-wide process to restructure its special education, Chapter 1, and at-risk services. Student needs were identified and decisions on reallocation of personnel and resources were made.

Cooperative teaching pairs (a regular education teacher and special education teacher) were formed. Planning time and support personnel permitted the cooperative pairs opportunities to develop and discuss their ideas about philosophy, grading, discipline, and curriculum modifications. This cooperative plan utilizing the expertise of both teachers allows students with mild and moderate disabilities, at risk, and with Chapter 1 needs to participate in regular classes. Miller offers 44 cooperatively taught classes in all skill and content areas.

Scheduling teachers, classes, and students is more complex with this model. Students are placed according to identified needs and by parent and teacher recommendation.

Major benefits of the cooperative teaching model include: more immediate feedback for learners, development of new teaching strategies, increased monitoring of assignment completion, simultaneous delivery of corrective methods and enrichments, decreased discipline problems, and personal and professional growth.

The elements that Miller has found crucial to the success of inclusive policies are the leadership of the principal, support of the school district via resources to maintain staff, staff development, and planning time.

Miller Middle School, 125 South 11th Street, Marshalltown, IA 50158.

MOSS ELEMENTARY SCHOOL
Metuchen, New Jersey

Moss Elementary School in Metuchen has 455 students attending kindergarten, 1st, and 2nd grade. Metuchen is a suburban town of 15,000 people, many of whom commute to New York City and Philadelphia. The school district has a student population of 1,600 and operates four schools: Moss; Campbell, a school for 3rd, 4th, and 5th graders; Edgar, a school for 6th and 7th graders; and Metuchen High School, a high school for 8th through 12th graders. The only prekindergarten class the school district offers is for children with disabilities.

Moss has 17 classroom teachers, 13 specialist teachers (art, music, resource room, special services, librarian, etc.), and 21 support staff, including classroom paraprofessionals, custodians, and lunch aides.

In January 1991, Moss enrolled a 7-year-old child with disabilities who had been attending a private school. Despite initial skepticism, the staff planned carefully for his inclusion. The experience was so successful that eight children who would otherwise have been placed in special classes are now attending regular classes at Moss. Because of the success of Moss's efforts, Metuchen no longer has any self-contained special education classes.

The team involved in helping Moss become an inclusive school is composed of a speech-language specialist, a school psychologist, a learning consultant, a social worker, a parent, a special education teacher, a grade-level teacher, and a paraprofessional. Team members meet regularly and with other pertinent staff members, such as the nurse and physical therapist.

The philosophy of the staff members and the school has become, "We Celebrate Diversity." Staff members have noticed with pleasure that students who otherwise would have been placed in separate classes have become active participants, not only in class but also in such social activities as scouting, sports teams, and birthday parties. Some of the other results of inclusive policies have been that classroom teachers, working collaboratively with other staff members, have developed confidence in their ability to meet the needs of students with disabilities. They share ideas and materials and have been encouraged by the high level of academic success of their students. They are also becoming skilled at using the services of other staff members. The art teacher, for example, works with the occupational therapist in art class. Parents have become more actively involved in the school, and all students have had the opportunity to experience the advantages of diversity.

Moss attributes its success to the leadership of its principal; the enthusiasm of the staff; extensive training and staff development; the development of a collaborative working style among staff members; and the support of the Board of Education, the Superintendent of Schools, and the Director of Special Services, who have paid for staff training, teacher assistants, planning time, and additional related services.

Moss Elementary School, Simpson Place, Metuchen, NJ 08840.

PETER A. REINBERG ELEMENTARY SCHOOL
Chicago, Illinois

Peter A. Reinberg Elementary School has 797 students in prekindergarten through 8th grade. It is on the northwest side of Chicago and serves a community of many first-generation Polish immigrants who make up about one quarter of the student body. Students identified as having disabilities make up 30% of Reinberg's student population.

Reinberg has 62 teachers, of whom 32 are special education teachers. In addition, it has a full-time social worker, a counselor, three speech-language therapists, an occupational therapist, and a speech-language assistant. A psychologist is in the school 4 days a week, and a nurse 3 days. There are 13 paraprofessionals and 11 child welfare attendants, whose primary job is to keep the children safe on the buses, but who are full members of the educational staff.

In 1988, Reinberg housed three completely separate programs: the regular education program, the hearing-impaired program, and the early childhood special education program. There was no communication among the programs; teachers did not even know each other's names.

The principal began to educate herself and her staff about inclusion. She arranged workshop discussions and visited or sent staff members to visit inclusive schools. One program was particularly helpful—the "Collaborative Leadership Development in Special Education for Principals" given by Leonard C. Burrello from Indiana University.

After the staff had explored the issue for a while, Reinberg began its first steps toward inclu-

sion. Co-teaching was adopted, in which a regular teacher and a special education teacher were paired to take responsibility for a heterogeneous class. By co-teaching, teachers have had opportunities to observe and intervene that were not available before. Teachers have also found co-teaching to be a way to reduce the isolation of classroom teaching.

Kindergartners with disabilities were the first to be included in regular classes, but now all grades, including preschool, are inclusive.

Teachers have rotated through job assignments, and often one of the teaching partners will progress with the students to the next grade, eliminating much of the strangeness of a new year.

Reinberg is still grappling with many of the issues posed by inclusion and is burdened by many of the problems of urban schools, including overcrowding and large numbers of students with limited proficiency in English.

Peter A. Reinberg Elementary School, 3425 North Major Avenue, Chicago, IL 60634.

WESTERLY HIGH SCHOOL
Westerly, Rhode Island

Westerly High School has 1,089 students in 8th through 12th grades. The town of Westerly, with a winter population of 22,000 and a summer population of 35,000, is in the southwestern corner of Rhode Island. Somewhat isolated from the main currents of Rhode Island, it has an independent and close-knit character. Italian Americans and Yankees have dominated the town, but there are growing Chinese and Hispanic populations. Defense, granite, and textile industries once provided economic stability to the region. Now, tourism and local small businesses provide the main employment opportunities.

The town operates four elementary schools (kindergarten through 4th grades), one middle school (5th, 6th, and 7th) and Westerly High School. Westerly has one principal, an assistant principal, 98 classroom teachers, and 12.4 other teachers, which include art, music, physical education, and library-media staff. In addition, it has 4.5 secretaries, 4.6 guidance counselors, and a building operations person.

Until a few years ago, Westerly students with disabilities were in self-contained classrooms from kindergarten through high school. A few had been placed in regular classes, notably two highly motivated, college-bound students who were blind. High school students with learning disabilities or behavioral problems generally were placed in the slow track, and eventually many were moved into segregated special education classes.

Three movements were merging to create this climate for change—support for shared decision making, support for staff development based on teachers' real needs, and an annual 2-day off-site conference for all teachers. By 1990, over 75% of the teachers had been trained in techniques of shared decision making, building teams, and reaching consensus.

By 1991, all students in Grades 8-12 were integrated into regular English and 8th-grade reading classes with a special education teacher and a regular teacher collaborating in the same classroom. Although the tracking system was still in place, and most of the students with disabilities continued to be placed in the slowest track because of poor reading and writing skills, significant changes were being made. Whole group instruction was abandoned and replaced with teacher-developed thematic units and packets that students could navigate at their own pace. With self-paced packets, students never feel hopelessly behind.

One of the biggest problems in the beginning was the lack of common planning time. During the first year, before there was money for substitute teachers, the department heads covered classes so that teachers could get together to plan. During the first year of inclusion, teachers spent most of the time getting used to working together and sorting out roles. Regular teachers found that strategies used in collaborative classrooms were so effective that they began using them in all their classes.

Westerly High School, 23 Ward Avenue, Westerly, RI 02891.

WORTON ELEMENTARY SCHOOL
Kent County, Maryland

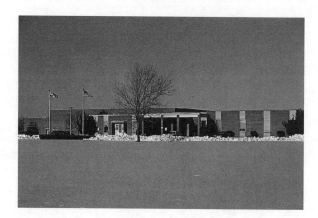

Worton Elementary School has 360 students. It is one of four elementary schools in Kent County, a rural area in Eastern Maryland that covers 284 square miles and has 2,600 students. In Kent County, the elementary schools contain prekindergarten through 4th grade, the three middle schools contain 5th through 8th grade, and the centrally located high school includes 9th through 12th grade.

Worton has 14 regular classroom teachers, 4 special education teachers, 4 special subjects teachers, 6 instructional assistants, and 1 occupational therapist, who is available 2 days per week.

Worton is the only elementary school in the county that houses a self-contained special education classroom for those students who need 15 or more hours of special services.

Children with disabilities have always been included in such daily routines as lunch, recess, homeroom, as well as music, art, physical education, and computer lab. But it was not until a mother asked for a more academic placement for her child who has disabilities that the school began an official policy of inclusion.

Worton has a philosophy of "quiet inclusion." That is, without announcing any new policies it has quietly included students with special needs in regular programs as appropriate.

Plans for inclusion were developed through the school improvement team, which includes the principal, a classroom teacher, a special education teacher, an instructional assistant, and a parent.

One of the strategies developed by the team pairs two classmates with special needs and similar ability levels as "buddies." A regular classroom teacher was paired with a special education teacher, and the two co-teach. The special education teacher keeps tabs on those children with special needs, but also teaches small and large groups of children. The co-teachers involved in inclusion were selected for their enthusiasm for the project and their classroom management skills.

At Worton, resource teachers and special education teachers provide extra assistance to students within regular classrooms, rather than pulling them out.

Worton uses whole group instruction, small group instruction, student pairing, and individual instruction—especially in the computer lab—as methods to meet the needs of each individual child.

Since the program's inception, several children with special needs have been incorporated into the regular classrooms, and all students have benefited from the interaction. Teachers who were once reluctant to receive students with disabilities are now eager to participate in the school's inclusive school program.

Worton Elementary School, 11085 Worton Road, Worton, MD 21678.

Policies and Position Statements on Inclusive Schools

Policies and Position Statements on Inclusive Schools

THE COUNCIL FOR EXCEPTIONAL CHILDREN (CEC) POLICY ON INCLUSIVE SCHOOLS AND COMMUNITY SETTINGS

The Council for Exceptional Children believes all children, youth, and young adults with disabilities are entitled to a free and appropriate education and/or services that lead to an adult life characterized by satisfying relations with others, independent living, productive engagement in the community, and participation in society at large. To achieve such outcomes, there must exist for all children, youth, and young adults a rich variety of early intervention, educational, and vocational program options and experiences. Access to these programs and experiences should be based on individual educational needs and desired outcomes. Furthermore, students and their families or guardians, as members of the planning team, may recommend the placement, curriculum option, and the exit document to be pursued.

CEC believes that a continuum of services must be available for all children, youth, and young adults. CEC also believes that the concept of inclusion is a meaningful goal to be pursued in our schools and communities. In addition, CEC believes children, youth, and young adults with disabilities should be served whenever possible in general education classrooms in inclusive neighborhood schools and community settings. Such settings should be strengthened and supported by an infusion of specially trained personnel and other appropriate supportive practices according to the individual needs of the child.

Policy Implications

Schools. In inclusive schools, the building administrator and staff with assistance from the special education administration should be primarily responsible for the education of children, youth, and young adults with disabilities. The administrator(s) and other school personnel must have available to them appropriate support and technical assistance to enable them to fulfill their responsibilities. Leaders in state/provincial and local governments must redefine rules and regulations as necessary, and grant school personnel greater authority to make decisions regarding curriculum, materials, instructional practice, and staffing patterns. In return for greater autonomy, the school administrator and staff should establish high standards for each child, youth, and young adult, and should be held accountable for his or her progress toward outcomes.

Communities. Inclusive schools must be located in inclusive communities; therefore, CEC invites all educators, other professionals, and family members to work together to create early intervention, educational, and vocational programs and experiences that are collegial, inclusive, and responsive to the diversity of children, youth, and young adults. Policymakers at the highest levels of state/provincial and local government, as well as school administration, also must support inclusion in the educational reforms they espouse. Further, the policymakers should fund programs in nutrition, early intervention, health care, parent education, and other social support programs that prepare all children, youth, and young adults to do well in school. There can be no meaningful school reform, nor inclusive schools, without funding of these key prerequisites. As important, there must be interagency agreements and collaboration with local governments and business to help prepare students to assume a constructive role in an inclusive community.

Professional Development. Finally, state/provincial departments of education, local educational districts, and colleges and universities must provide high-quality preservice and continuing professional development experiences that prepare all general educators to work effectively with children, youth, and young adults representing a wide range of abilities and disabilities, experiences, cultural and linguistic backgrounds, attitudes, and expectations. Moreover, special educators should be trained with an emphasis on their roles in inclusive schools and community settings. They also must learn the importance of establishing ambitious goals for their students and of using appropriate means of monitoring the progress of children, youth, and young adults.

The Council for Exceptional Children. (1994). *CEC Policies for Delivery of Services to Exceptional Children.* Reston, VA: Author. Adopted by the Delegate Assembly of The Council for Exceptional Children in April 1993.

NATIONAL ASSOCIATION OF STATE BOARDS OF EDUCATION

Resolution 94-6: Equal Educational Opportunity

B. Students with Special Needs

1. To ensure equal educational opportunities, services should be provided for special student needs. Learning programs should identify and address the individual needs and learning styles of all students, including those who are disabled, disadvantaged, migrant, gifted or talented, parenting or pregnant, minority or of limited English proficiency.

2. State boards should ensure that policies are developed and implemented which guarantee that all students are educated in school environments that include rather than exclude them. School environments encompass all curricular, co-curricular, and extracurricular programs and activities. Inclusion means that all children must be educated in supported, heterogenous, age-appropriate, natural, child-focused school environments for the purpose of preparing them for full participation in our diverse and integrated society.

National Association of State Boards of Education. (1994). Resolution 94-6: Equal Educational Opportunity.

NATIONAL ASSOCIATION OF ELEMENTARY SCHOOL PRINCIPALS (NAESP) PLATFORM 94-95

1. THE CHILD

A. The Child

Focus on the Child

NAESP believes that the child is the focal point of the educational process. It is the shared responsibility of the principal, instructional staff, parents, and community to facilitate the direction and use of available skills and resources toward helping each child develop a positive self-image and to strengthen feelings of self-worth in assisting each child to experience success in society.

The Association believes the primary focus in education should be on pupils rather than teachers, on learning rather than teaching, and that the professional assessment of educational outcomes be based on multidimensional indicators of quality.

Therefore, NAESP urges all groups involved in the educational process of children to work in unity for the total development of the child by providing opportunities by which each child may realize his/her fullest potential. ('71, '72, '86, '94)

Maintaining Children's Positive Self-Concepts

NAESP is aware of and appreciates the efforts of educational agencies to provide programs for children who need special instructional help. However, the Association deplores the demeaning language used to designate the population for whom the programs are designed. The use of terms such as "culturally deprived," "underprivileged," "mentally retarded," and "reluctant learner" negates the positive impact of the program.

Guidelines that mandate the grouping of children who are so identified result in **de facto** segregation, the realization of which is obvious to the children.

NAESP urges all federal, state, and local agencies entrusted with the welfare of children to be aware of the harmful effects of labeling that tend to destroy a child's self-concept, and to take the action necessary to correct this situation. ('79, '90)

B. RIGHTS

Equal Education Opportunity

NAESP supports efforts that promote the right of every child to an equal education opportunity regardless of ethnicity, handicap, race, religious belief, sex, or socioeconomic status. ('82, '92)

Student Disabilities

NAESP urges school systems to provide educational programs that will permit all children to develop their abilities and aptitudes to the fullest extent possible.

The Association endorses and supports the concepts embodied in the Individuals with Disabilities Education Act and Section 504 of the Rehabilitation Act of 1973, with emphasis in early identification beginning at birth, guaranteeing that all youngsters, irrespective of handicapping and/or health conditions, are entitled to a free appropriate education in the least restrictive environment.

NAESP supports inclusion of special education students, as appropriate, in regular classrooms with their peers in their neighborhood schools. To facilitate the successful inclusion of special education students, NAESP recognizes that appropriate financial resources, staff development, and support services must follow the child with disabilities.

The Association also recognizes that compliance with legal mandates presents additional managerial and administrative duties that impede the orderly and efficient delivery of educational services to all students.

NAESP supports continuation and expansion of related services to local districts by appropriate state and community service agencies. Additional state and federal financial support is imperative for local school districts to comply with the provisions of these laws. ('76, '77, '79, '90, '91, '93, '94)

National Association of Elementary School Principals. (1994). NAESP Platform 94-95, pages 1–2.

National Education Association (NEA) Policy Statement on Appropriate Inclusion

The National Education Association is committed to equal educational opportunity, the highest quality education, and a safe learning environment for all students. The Association supports and encourages **appropriate inclusion. Appropriate inclusion** is characterized by practices and programs which provide for the following on a sustained basis:

- A full continuum of placement options and services within each option. Placement and services must be determined for each student by a team that includes all stakeholders and must be specified in the Individualized Education Program (IEP).
- Appropriate professional development, as part of normal work activity, of all educators and support staff associated with such programs. Appropriate training must also be provided for administrators, parents, and other stakeholders.
- Adequate time, as part of the normal school day, to engage in coordinated and collaborative planning on behalf of all students.
- Class sizes that are responsive to student needs.
- Staff and technical assistance that is specifically appropriate to student and teacher needs.

Inclusion practices and programs which lack these fundamental characteristics are inappropriate and must end.

Adopted by NEA Board of Directors, May 1994.

National School Boards Association (NSBA) Inclusion Issues

At the local level we see increasing efforts to include students with disabilities in the general curriculum. These efforts are likely to continue. **But greater inclusion does not require any changes in federal law.** IDEA already requires that students be educated in the "least restrictive environment" and any changes in the law are likely to produce significant disruption at the local level and unnecessary and costly new litigation.

Inclusion can work effectively for large numbers of students with disabilities while enriching the classroom experience of all students. But for inclusion to work effectively frequently requires extensive teacher training, additional classroom aides, and in some cases, the purchase of expensive additional classroom technology.

To promote greater inclusion without providing the resources to make it work offers a false promise of improved opportunities for students with disabilities, and the real possibility of disruptions in the learning environment. The federal government needs to make the resources available to local school districts so more inclusive special education programming, where appropriate, can be highly successful.

Likewise, we must understand that full inclusion is not appropriate for some students with disabilities. For students with disabilities who require extensive individualized assistance or who do not have sufficiently well developed social skills, instruction in the general curriculum may not be beneficial. Many teachers and disability advocates share our belief that full inclusion is not always an educationally sound strategy.

Testimony of Boyd Boehlje, President, National School Boards Association, before the House Subcommittee on Select Education and Civil Rights, July 19, 1994.